The Four Villages

Lynemouth, Ellington, Cresswell & Linton

by Neil Taylor

Acknowledgements

The following people and organisations have generously donated either text, photos, images or discs in the production of this book. This is greatly appreciated and I make a point of a personal thanks wherever possible.

Milburn Douglas, Alan Simpson, Margaret Simpson, Ray Ditchburn, Alan Reed, Doris Teasdale, Connie Groves, Jean Strother, Jessie Rich, Ray Brotherton, Brian Lonsdale, Dave Hindmarsh, Clarry Green, Andrew Gooding, Lynemouth Resource Centre, Bob Weddle, John Robinson, Ella Little, Jean and Jack Tubby, Marjorie Neave, Leita Collins, Elaine Weallans, Charlie Sweet, Kathleen Holdroyd, Joss Hanson, John & Kath Robson, Rene Teasdale, Joanne Fairfax, Lindsay Lamb, Mary Fairbairn, Barry Mead, Bob Snaith, Bill Redford, Mike & Lorna Kirkup, Mary and Peter Willis, Violet Carruthers, Jim Pegg's testimony, Sandra Cresswell, Ann & Jack Patrick, Les Hallowell, Ian Leech, Stuart Chapman,William Leech Campus, Wellway Surgery, Betty Freeman, Tom Hewitson, Kit Miller, John Graham, Olive Graham, Tom Morris, Olive Brown, Maisie Cuthbertson, Gerald Tait, Ray Dunn, Ellington Football Club, Iris Evans, Jo Tipple, Trevor Walker.

Bibliography

Beamish Museum, Northumberland County Archives Woodhorn,
British Newspaper Archives, Lynemouth School Records.

Dedication

To my boyhood pals – Henry Cleverley, Clarry Green and Alan Dickinson.

A lifetime of memories to treasure.

Previous page: Two fine young men employed in the sinking operations at Ellington Colliery from 1909-13. The Telford brothers are seen here in typical early sinking attire of waistcoat, cranky flannen, gaiters and boots.

Front cover, top photo: Cresswell Church members trip by charabanc in the 1920s, pictured outside Ellington Vicarage. *Bottom photo:* Lynemouth School Gala in 1957 with children and parents outside the Welfare Field.

Back cover, top photo: Cresswell women and children hauling in the lifeboat after a mission in 1935. *Bottom photo:* Linton School during the miners strike in 1926 with helpers and children at the soup kitchen

Copyright Neil Taylor 2015

First published in 2015 by

Summerhill Books
PO Box 1210, Newcastle upon Tyne NE99 4AH

www.summerhillbooks.co.uk

email: summerhillbooks@yahoo.co.uk

ISBN: 978-1-906721-99-2

Introduction

The time to record my final chapter of the history and many changes that have occurred in and around the Lynemouth, Linton, Ellington and Cresswell area is now – to complete what is most definitely a labour of love for me. Fond memories make for enthusiastic research and writing, and one thing I know for certain, I have never forgotten my roots.

History tells us that there are strong and definite ties that linked the villages. Agriculture, mining, schooling, religion, leisure and social connections all played a part in this. For the people of the four villages even closer ties might have been established had a proposed new town been built between Ellington and Lynemouth in the 1950s. Broadlyne was the name of the scheme to incorporate new miners coming into the area and to provide work for women through light industry. A grand scheme on a 221 acre site to include 4,000 new houses had provision for not only an industrial estate but also a shopping centre, primary and secondary schools, a Roman Catholic Church and a welfare centre. It was neighbouring town councils who opposed this plan at a public enquiry on the grounds that they would lose 4,000 of their population and a lowering of their rateable value. However, permission was eventually granted for the construction of 800 houses but the whole scheme was finally shelved in 1956 owing to the uncertain future of the coal industry. The rejection of the Broadlyne scheme also resulted in stopping the building of a new 600 pupil secondary school at Lynemouth. This school being opened at Newbiggin in 1963.

The villages are different now both socially and economically. This has happened mainly because of the closure of the collieries at Linton, Lynemouth and Ellington and more recently the devestating impact of the shutting down of Rio Tinto Alcan Lynemouth Aluminium Smelter.

Yet a link to our industrial heritage still survives as the colliery houses and cottages still stand in Lynemouth, Linton and Ellington Colliery with many of the offspring of the original families still in residence. Sadly this has not happened in many of the local pit villages such as North Seaton, Widdrington, East Chevington, Radcliffe and Stobswood. These old coal mining communities are but a tiny fraction of the many in the county whose residents have had to move on to pastures new and start again when their villages were demolished

There are folk out there in the four villages who are moving with the times and have a real passion to see them thrive – working hands on to make this happen. Many of them are shown or recorded within this publication.

This book contains many photos and sketches that have never previously been published. In many cases it compares the old with the new. I sincerely hope the content represents a fair reflection of past events and the changes that have occurred in the area over the years. If it gives you as much enjoyment as I have had in producing this publication, stirs the nostalgia within you, or fills you with a sense of pride, then I will have gone some way towards achieving my goal.

Neil Taylor
Ellington
2015

Ellington Institute Committee in the 1920s with the caretaker and a little girl seated in front with her pet dog.

Looking Bac[k]

The history of the area around the mouth of the River [...]
mists of time. Artefacts found in an archaeological di[g ...]
Strawberry Hill as locals would come to know it, pro[...]
ancestors inhabited this site. Flints were also found t[...]
near to where the course of the Lyne Burn used to ru[...]
Newbiggin Bay. 'Linmith' as it was known then woul[...]
lives of those people who relied on the forest, shore li[...]
and access to food sources.

Prior to the arrival of the Ashington Coal Company [...]
area in the early 20th century, the land was purely ag[...]
small scale by tenanted farmers at Dene House, Lyner[...]

Handwritten note:
Artefacts found.
Lyne Hill 1920] River Lyne.
Strawberry Hill]
Hunter - gatherer inhabited this site.
Flints found to the South on Newbiggin Moor
Lynemouth pre 20th century
Agricultural on small scale by tenanted farmers at Dene House.
Lynemouth Farm and Lynefield.
P4.

Lyne Bay

The Beach, Lynemouth. 8537

The river estuary as it was before the start of coal tipping along the bay. The problem of dumping colliery waste from the two pits was a major headache for the coal authorities. At Ellington there was waste tipping on the pit site from the early years of production and there certainly was an unsightly pit heap at the east side of the colliery. Lynemouth Colliery, sunk much later and not producing coal until the 1930s, saw less of waste tipping at their site.

A happy group of Lynemouth residents enjoying a day out in 1948 at that famous picnic spot by the mouth of the River Lyne. Back row: Jean Herron, Eddie O'Keefe, Annie Simpson, Wilson Meredith, Mrs Meredith. Front row: Mrs Lane, Mrs O'Keefe, Mrs Gray with son Denis, Jim Simpson, Freddy Gray. Forefront: Peggy Holland with son Alan, Margaret Simpson.

In the 1950s the National Coal Board had taken over the Strawberry Hill area, removed sandbanks, laid railway lines to the site from Lynemouth Colliery and constructed two disposal point beltways which deposited waste material from Ellington and Lynemouth Collieries onto the foreshore. The belt on the left is in operation tipping waste and the bulldozers below levelling it out.

A view from the belt head shows its position on the hill in relation to Lynemouth. The Church of St Aidan and its vicarage plus West Market street shops can just be seen in the background on the right across the River Lyne.

Coal from seams at sea bed level have been harvested from the beach for hundreds of years. The monks of Lindisfarne in the 7th century were familiar with what they called 'se coles'. With the tipping of vast amounts of colliery waste, collecting and selling the coal became a way of life for many people. It was backbreaking work as this picture shows of a man with sacks of coal loaded on his bike coming off Boghall Beach.

A south easterner is the best wind to rough up the sea and bring coals into Lyne Bay which brought out the sea coalers with their horses and carts to be filled with the black diamonds and hauled off the beach to be stored or sold to locals. Rob and Jacky Brown shown here were two of the regular coalers.

After decades of mining waste from Ellington and Lynemouth Collieries being dumped on the foreshore the area is now slowly reverting back to nature. The moving of the travellers' camp from the dunes to the River Lyne site meant a partial clearing of the area. The banks either side of the river estuary are once again carpeted with wild flowers in late spring and summer, while the clifftop area from river to Snab

Point Quarry is slowly recovering with patches of thyme evident once again among the rough dune grass. This is a poem I penned after one of my regular visits to the bay in March 2014.

By the Edge of the Sea by Neil Taylor

A snug little bay once shot with colliery waste is alive again.
From river mouth to Snab Point rocks a ribbon of silver sand
threads through a highline of weathered sandstone cliffs and down
to the edge of the sea. Ringed Plovers nested here last summer and
raised two broods above the tideline.

First day of Spring I am clifftop and couched on a bed of thyme.
The stiff winged Fulmars are back from their wintering out over
the high seas, they ghost around the cliff edges on curious winds
hatched out at the swell of the tide. I am comfortable here in this
my place of big sky and open water.

An ancient place where a century ago they measured time
by the flints dug from under the clifftop marram grass and an old
fossilised tree hewn out of the seabanks. And there high up locked
between shattered sandstone measures, a two foot seam of outcrop coal
that we had worked in the strike of seventy two.

Today I am back to watch the Fulmars fly, they like me have
heritage here. Mine is well defined, given up by the sea
twice every day and printed out on the tideline. A curve of shucked
and sieved sea bed coal, a necklace of black diamonds strung out
around the neck of the bay.

Lynemouth Township

The oldest buildings in the original Lynemouth Parish are Dene House, Lynemouth Farm and Linefield Farm. Dene House is shown on old maps and dates from at least the 18th century. However, Lynemouth Farmhouse has brought up some real questions on date of construction since Julia and Barry Say began renovating the property. The Watson family who owned North Seaton Hall are known to have lived here as did the Atkinson family who owned much of Lynemouth during the 19th century.

Julia and Barry Say at the front door of Lynemouth Farmhouse during restoration work in 2011. The front of the farmhouse is facing south and next to the original old Lynemouth road, named Jacks Lonnen, that is still in use behind Lynemouth Welfare and terminated at Woodhorn Mill. This is probably 18th century but the back of the house, facing north adjacent to Queen Street council houses and facing Park Road, shows evidence of a Northumbrian longhouse from the 16th century. Also there is evidence of previous buildings having stood in that area. There are also records of a manor house being established there.

The first record of Ashington Coal Company having use of the farmhouse was in 1916 when the Ellington Colliery pit manager, Mr Stanley Hunter, was residing there. From then, until the 1960s, it saw a succession of Ellington managers and coal board officials come and go. In 1922 came the longest serving Ellington Colliery manager, Mr A.E. Holliday, known to locals as the colonel because of his dress and bearing. He was prominent in village life, serving as a school governor, a St Aidan's Church warden and an early member of the Parish Council. In 1945, local man Bill Wilkinson resided there for seven years before Mr W. Nelson arrived in 1952 and stayed until 1954. Then came Mr Willis for two years and Jim Graham, whose tenure was for only one year until 1958. Mr G.E. Hiller arrived in 1959 and stayed until 1961 when Mr W.S. Davison arrived to live there as the last coal board tenant.

The well discovered at the back door of the farmhouse. Before water was piped into Lynemouth to supply the new village in 1921, this was the means of obtaining a source. It has been proven that the area was littered with wells just like this.

Building a Model Village

The Ashington Coal Company decided to build a modern village at Lynemouth from 1921 with a view to opening up a new coal mine in the immediate vicinity. This new enclave would be very different from the old style houses they built at Ashington and Ellington Colliery. The whole scheme was anticipated to include 1,500 houses. There were five types of Coal Company houses built, ranging from two to five bedroom properties erected in blocks of from eight to fourteen. A garden with an area of 60 feet by 20 feet and with avenues of trees planted 20 yards apart between the blocks and the road. The street names came as the houses were built in alphabetical order such as Albion Road, Boland Road and Chester Square. The name Chester may have come from the village overseer at that time who was a Mr Chester. It is not until the building of Fenham Road that we see most of the streets being built and named after towns, districts or villages but still retaining the alphabet system.

Circa 1922 and looking east showing the first houses of Chester Square and Boland Road nearing completion on the left of picture and Coal Company employees bringing up supplies by horse and cart from the holding depot on the West Green. Far right, the building of the odd numbered houses of Dalton Avenue are also well underway.

Looking west towards Ellington Colliery. In the foreground a small gauge railway was laid around the whole Lynemouth site to transport building materials as work progressed. The tubs that ran along these rails were a mecca for young boys after workmen had finished for the day. They would whiz round the site inside the tubs often coming to grief along the way.

A view north west towards Ellington Colliery with its pit chimney smoking in the background and Lynemouth Dene and Chugdon Wood featured back right of picture. The building of the model village at an advanced stage of construction.

This row of twelve houses was built in 1925 especially for pit officials and those clientele retained by the Ashington Coal Company. Standing high above the River Lyne looking west to Dene House and on to Ellington, this row was aptly named Lyne Terrace. The first occupants were Mr Leithead, an engineer at no 1, with architect T. Bell living in no 2 while future Linton School headmaster, Edwin Harrison, resided at no 12. The rail tracks were used by engines to haul away wagon loads of building site rubbish. Chester Square can be seen in the background. The road to the right leads to the top of the bridge that spanned the Ellington to Lynemouth road and the railway line. Consequently it became the norm that we youngsters living in houses at the north side of the bridge always said that those people living in homes at the south side of the bridge were from 'Ower the other side of the Line.'

The even numbered houses of Dalton Avenue as they were in 1925. My home for many years was number 28 the first large house at the beginning of the second block in the centre of picture. This postcard shows the newly made up gardens and picket fence with hedges planted behind. Trees were planted by Ashington Coal Company every twenty yards along the edge of the footpaths. The houses on the right opposite are the odd numbered Dalton Avenue houses.

Ashington Coal Company's Oven Baked Bricks

It was in 1948 when our family moved from Eden Terrace into a large five bedroom end terraced house in Dalton Avenue. The downstairs rooms could be kept warm even in the depths of winter with a coal fire roaring in the grate. The bedroom fires were never used owing to smoke problems and on cold nights it was not uncommon to find ice on the inside of the windows. My sister, brother and myself were always cold in bed; we could hear the wind whipping through the gap between the two end houses and the windows would shake and rattle.

One night just before bedtime my mother called us over to the fireplace and opened the oven door set in the big black-leaded range. Inside were three ACC bricks which she wrapped in separate blankets handing one to each of us. They were well baked and hot even under the wrapping. After mother tucked us up in our beds I remember the joy of placing my feet on the brick and feeling the warmth spread through my body. In the cold dark winter nights, we never went to bed without our brick.

Living By The Railway Line by Leita Collins (Russell)

I was born in 1943 in Ingleby Terrace on the south side of the railway line that split Lynemouth in two. My dad Bill was an engine driver for the Coal Board and he often passed by when his tanky was pulling coal trains down to Lynemouth Washery. I remember sometimes he would stop outside our back garden which was only ten yards from the railway line and let me ride in the train and sound the whistle.

We lived next door to the Clancey family – Billy, Emma and daughter Mary and they were great neighbours. It was the time of share what you had and help was just a knock at the door away.

My mother had a strict routine on weekdays. Monday was washing day, Tuesdays ironing, bedrooms on Wednesday and living room cleaned on Thursdays. Friday was clean the back yard and windows day and it all happened between endless cups of tea with neighbours.

A lad named Colin Birch worked as an order boy for the Store (Co-op) and called at our house on Friday for our grocery order which would then be delivered on the Saturday by a man called Jack who drove a horse and cart and then a motor wagon.

The railway line that split the village with Albion Terrace houses on the left not built until 1947 and the colliery houses of Ingleby Terrace to the right of the tracks, built from 1924.

I woke up one morning feeling really ill when at primary school and I was diagnosed with Scarlet Fever. Doctor Skene said that I must have contracted the illness from Colin as we were the only cases in Lynemouth at that time. My mother refused to send me to the Pity Me Isolation Hospital at North Seaton and so no one was allowed in our house for three months and I lost four months schooling.

Christmas was always a joyous but busy time as the week before our house was cleaned from top to bottom and sometimes decorated. My dad always delivered the Christmas tree by tanky and threw it over our garden hedge and sometimes a bag of veg. Where they came from I never new. I remember one occasion when my dad, who had just woken up after foreshift, said to my mother, 'Me and the bairn want to put the Christmas tree up.'

Mother said, 'No Billy, you can't – the room is not ready yet.'

He looked at me and said, 'Well we want it up. It won't tek long.' Out he went and dragged the five foot tree inside. I could see from mother's eyes that she was becoming angry as she looked at him and me. He went outside again and came back with a bucket of coal as mother said, 'What's that for like?'

'For the tree man. It'll not stand up itself.'

'You need soil or sand man. It'll not stand up in that.'

'This'll be okay. Tell is when it's straight' as he plonked it in the bucket. Looking pleased with his efforts he said to me, 'Gan and get the toy things pet' and as I turned around the whole lot collapsed on mother's freshly scrubbed lino floor. There was silence for a few seconds before mother jumped up and threw the tree and then the bucket of coal right across the room.

It was at that point Emma Clancey walked in with a pot of tea in her hands saying. 'Aave just made the tea' … and when she saw the mess she just turned around and walked out gobasmacked. Mother followed with a parting shot at dad, 'Get that cleaned up, Billy!'

Dad was a loveable character and every two years he had a load of horse manure dropped at the corner of the street and mother and me had to wheel it round to the garden. Why he did this I never knew as he never grew anything and mother was always asking him when he was going to start. His answer was 'When we got him a left handed spade!'

One thing I remember well is going around the streets with Joe and Mary Pollard checking dustbin lids to see if folk had left potato peelings or bits of food which could be boiled up and used to feed the Pollard's pig that they kept at the allotments. Joe would pull a wooden trailer while Mary and me filled it with scraps.

I loved those days when everybody seemed equal in monetary terms and had time for one another. Walks in the Dene, Primroses and Bluebells, Pictures at the Tute, Saturday night at the Arcade Dance and many more simple things – that was enough for most of us in those days.

This photo shows 'the other side of the line.' Little Alan Simpson in 1925 riding a mint of a bike in the back street between Fenham Road and Guilford Square looking down to Ingleby Terrace. The Simpson family were among the first residents in the village and Alan's siblings are still around to this day.

Boland Road, Lynemouth.   6832

In the 1920s Robert Johnson travelled the county taking topographical photographs and often visited the new village of Lynemouth. Here is a scene from the West Green. In the foreground is Mr Johnson's car alongside one of the young trees that were planted along the avenues and became a feature of the Lynemouth streets. Behind the car is what was Patrick's shop and later Billy Mann's with the offshoot used by Wilson Cochrane as a men's barbers.

Extreme left is Ingleby Terrace at the other side of the railway line. Boland Road is on the right then the West Bridge across the main road and railway. The hut in the centre of picture was used by Ashington Coal Company who employed electrician, Mr Bamford, who gave out new light bulbs to Lynemouth tenants.

The West Green has been a bit of a puzzle for some time as to why it was never built on and why the building of houses in the short row of Boland Road was not continued over the green to match up with those of the long row of Boland Road houses opposite. Well there is an answer. The colliery houses in this area were among the first to be built and ACC left the green area with a view to building a community hall for the residents. However, with the construction of the Institute from 1925 and all its social facilities proving so popular with the locals, it was thought not necessary to have another facility in the village.

Over the years the green has played host to a fish shop and play park. Interest had been shown from other sources to build on the land but nothing materialised. In the very early years, it was a ready made football, cricket field and play area for youngsters from the west end of the village. Today, it stands vacant, just as it did all those years ago.

Living with Wildlife

Many of the colliery houses were infested with blackbeetles which we always called Blackclocks. They were big shiny black beetles that loved to hide in the cupboards next to the fireplace. My dad said they worked night shift like he did as they were rarely seen in the daytime. They were ugly with a hard body armour that made a crunching noise when stood on. Sprays and powder were used to get rid of them, this worked for a while but they soon returned bringing their sons, daughters, aunts, uncles and anyone else that wanted to come.

I remember one of my dad's tricks that he used when he came home after working nightshift. He would quietly open the backdoor and tiptoe over to the living room before switching on the light. The beetles would scatter and make for their holes with my dad racing after them swotting as many as he could with his slipper. One of his favourite sayings when asked about the black beauties was this: 'Noo Aa divint mind seeing one or two, but when yi come yem and tha heving a tea party on the mat then that's teking liberties.'

'The Tute'

The building of Lynemouth Welfare Institute began in 1925 and these photos show the main hall at the rear almost complete while work goes on at the front to finalise the snooker room, gymnasium and first floor reading rooms. Described on completion as one of the finest Georgian style buildings of its kind in the North, it was to be the centre of the mining families' social activities in the new model village.

The refurbishment of the Institute was part funded by the Coalfields Regeneration Trust, the Coal Industry Social Welfare Organisation, the Federation Breweries and Newcastle Breweries. The entire ground floor being refurbished and part altered to provide a more modern and relaxing atmosphere. The main hall concert room, seen

here after refurbishment, was transformed. This hall originally catered for roller skating and then became known as the Gaiety Theatre which housed the Operatic Society and then the Lynemouth Cinema.

Pictured right are some of the hardworking committee of Lynemouth Welfare Institute and guest at the opening. On the left are: Anne Nelson, Lottie Scott, Arthur Fawkes and Alan Clark. To the right are: Hugh Scott, Carol Bennett, Sadie Williamson, John Brannen and Leo Wilson, from the construction company.

Leek growing and showing is still a highly competitive hobby, keeping up the traditions of the old mining communities. Committee men, Bill Thompson, left, and Tot Fairfax, right, with members gather to discuss the show judges' results at the end of the judging at Lynemouth Institute in 2012.

Lynemouth and Ellington Institutes still have thriving horticultural shows with produce being displayed in September. Standing in front of their exhibits in the flower section at Lynemouth Institute are prizewinners Mary Taylor and Alison Bell.

Shops and Business

By 1929 the village had attracted various traders to ply their business interests and here is a list as shown in Kelly's Directory: Ashington Co-op; James Chrisp Newsagent; Eras Harbottle, Insurance Agent 26, Albion Terrace; Lloyds Bank; Moyes Fish Shop; Welfare Hall; John George Purvis, Hairdresser 3, West Market Street; Thomas Skene Doctor 13, Albion Terrace; W. Smail Butcher of 3, West Market Street; M. Wilkinson Newsagent Albion Terrace; Sylvester Strong Lynemouth Hotel; Thomas Hume Policeman; Miss Knutton District Nurse; Leveo Guazelli Confectionery 5, West Market Street; Wm Foster Boot and Shoe repairer Albion Terrace.

The Lynemouth Cobblers

Bill Redford, born at Lynemouth in 1937 and now living in Australia, sent a message and photo asking for information about his father's former cobblers shop. The photo right shows his father, Jack Redford, at his workbench repairing boots at his Albion Road shop. Bill reckons it is an early to mid 1930s picture as his father retired owing to ill health before he was born. I found Jack Redford's name in the Kellys Directory of 1939, listed as a 'Boot and Shoe Repairer at Albion Road, Lynemouth.'

Prior to Jack owning the premises, it was owned in 1929 by Wm Foster also a Boot and Shoe Repairer. In the 1940s and 50s, Basil Morris was in attendance there, also listed as a Boot and Shoe Repairer. The premises was then taken over by Denis and Lilian Stafford who traded for many years as newagents and general dealers. The little offshoot attached, served as a bookmakers shop and then a hairdressers. Bill was happy to know the Albion Road premises are still standing today and in use as a private residence.

Jack Redford seen in the 1930s at his workbench in the Albion Road Boot and Shoe Repairers shop.

By 1939 there were new traders appearing in the village which was still under the umbrella of Ashington Coal Company and represented by R.L. Booth: John Clavering PO and General Dealer; John Dodd Dentist operating from the doctor's surgery; Wm Easton Newsagent at Albion Terrace; Chris Graham Confectioner Albion Terrace; John Mcoy at the Welfare; R.J. Patrick General Dealer; J. Redford Boot Repairer; Winnie Stafford Confectionery; Wm Watson Hairdresser Albion Terrace.

Basil Morris took over the Albion Terrace Boot Repairers business and then Denis Stafford occupied the premises in the 1950s running a newsagency. In the offshoot adjoining this, a hairdresser was resident before Jimmy

The large premises on the left of Albion Terrace was the home of William Easton who ran a newsagency and general dealers from here and commissioned a company to photograph and publish postcards of Lynemouth village. The building on the right, now demolished, was a Post Office and general dealers.

Kindley occupied the building and started up as a bookmaker in the 1960s. Opposite here, Wilkinson's shop was taken over by general dealer Mr Archibald and then by John Robinson. The West Market Street shops have changed hands many times over the years. Moffatt ran the chemists for many years and Charlton opened a bakery while Harry Charlton occupied premises in the row before moving to Dene House. Moyes ran the early fish and chip shop before Cole, who ran the business there after the war years. Jim Morrison ran a successful business at the Post Office which also twinned as a grocery store for a number of years. Billy Mann ran a painting and decorating business from his shop beside the West Bridge and Wilson Cochrane used the offshoot as a barbers.

Elsie Nichol used premises at the rear of West Market Street chemists as a ladies hairdressing salon and later Sharon's Salon was trading behind Pearson's Stores. Dick Nicholson opened a garage in 1969 at the end of West Market Street which was later used as a Post Office and now a popular angling shop. The Albion Road newsagents, formerly Easton's, has been run as a convenience store by Mr Cullen for many years. The old Co-op hardware premises is now a furniture store owned by Peter Johnson and the chemists shop run by the Burdon family. Patrick's grocery shop is now a convenience store.

15

This area was the open air meeting place for early Lynemouth Primitive Methodists before their chapel was built in 1927. Now an angling shop is sited here and growing ever popular with a prime position near the sea attracting fishermen on their way to the local fishing hot spots of Lyne Bay and Cresswell. The offshoot, once Dick Nicholson's garage workshop, started trading as a general dealers and operated a washing and cleaning service and then began trading as the 'Cabbage Patch' selling fruit and veg.

Staff and customers celebrating the shop opening. A little different to the latter day range of mostly food outlets in West Market Street. The Lynemouth Anglers have also found time to run a football team operating under the same name and playing in the North Northumberland League.

Short, Back and Sides

Wilson Cochrane was Lynemouth's barber during the 1940s, 50s and 60s. He cut hair slowly and in one style only and that was short all over. This suited the pitmen of the village well as they had to wear pit hats and sweated a lot under these. One day in the 50s when trendy styles were coming into fashion, a young lad who was visiting the village went in and asked for a Tony Curtis cut. After Wilson had finished cutting he held up a mirror for the boy to view. 'That's not a Tony Curtis cut man!' and Wilson promptly replied, 'It is if he ever comes in here bonny lad.'

His premises were a little offshoot next to Patrick's shop on Albion Road where Gills shop is now trading and the little room was always full of men and boys. Lots of men smoked them days and there was no extractor fan to clear the air. I remember watching the smoke curling in drifts around the place which I later christened 'Hernandos Hideaway'. Wilson never hurried and conducted a small lending library from the same room between one haircut and the next.

Smarty – The Paper Shop Dog

Old Jimmy lived in Dalton Avenue and owned an aptly named sheepdog called Smarty. The dog was highly intelligent, performing tricks that were beyond the scope of most other canines. Smarty was devoted to old Jim and seemed to possess a sixth sense as to what he wanted him to do.

One Sunday morning after a night socialising at Lynemouth Social Club, Jim was still worse the wear from the drink. He said to Smarty, 'Gan and get wor Sunday paper from Easton's paper shop bonny lad and bring it back here.' Smarty loped off and Jim settled down on the couch with a cup of tea. After an hour the dog had not returned home and Jim became anxious not knowing why Smarty was away so long. He set off for the newsagents at the end of the street and when he arrived and opened the shop door, there was Smarty sitting in the middle of the floor shaking his head from side to side. Mr Easton the newsagent was looking red faced and rather perplexed. 'What's the matter wi Smarty, Easton, aa sent him here for the Sunday paper.'

'Whats the matter, aal tell you what's the matter Jimmy, aave run oot of Sunday Suns and he wiinit tek the News Of The World.'

Lynemouth Colliery

A viaduct was dug in 1925 to take rail traffic to the site of the proposed new colliery which was to be sited near the sea at Lynemouth and a road overbridge constructed next to Lynemouth Institute. Here is a fine picture of the work in progress looking down to the sea. Strawberry Hill, Lynemouth's favourite picnic venue adjacent to the mouth of the River Lyne, can be seen top left of picture.

Five unique pictures from William Gibson's collection showing the start of the building of surface infrastructure.

The first Lynemouth
Colliery Shaft Tower after
erection. Sinking began in
1927 but the first coals to
come out of the new pit
were drawn up the
Woodhorn Colliery shafts.
This shaft was not in full
use until 1934. It was the
seven month coal stoppage
of 1926 that delayed the
sinking of Lynemouth.

The 1940s and the
pit expanding and
producing, with
the viaduct on the
left of picture
railed up and
transporting coal.
The wagons on the
right are standing
at Lynemouth
Battery ready to
move under the
coal loading areas
of the pit with the
two shaft towers
seen in the rear.

Recreation time for these colliery electricians when they were bussed away for a day at
the races in 1950. In this case the venue was Ayr. Jollification and drink would be on
the menu for many of these men taking the opportunity to forget about life
underground for a while. Lynemouth men, Ralph Clark and Norman Campbell, are
standing sixth and eighth from the left.

First Aid and membership of the St John Ambulance Brigade was actively encouraged by the owners of the Ashington Collieries Group from the early 20th century. Later colliery teams would compete against each other in the various areas of the National Coal Board. Lynemouth and Ellington Collieries were highly successful during the 1950s and 60s and members of both teams are seen here with trainer Wilfy Dick front left of photo.

Lynemouth Colliery about 1950 from the east prior to modernisation showing the marshalling yards in front of the coal screening plant and the pony field on the left of the main complex.

The new coal washery plant at Lynemouth Colliery built at the time of the pit's modernisation programme in the 1950s. A massive investment by the Coal Board both on the surface and underground was intended to make Lynemouth Colliery the Coal Board's 'Jewel in the Crown' – mining vast reserves of coal way out under the North Sea using the most up to date mining technology.

Included in the surface modernisation was a new hi-tech storehouse and workshops in the colliery yard.

A modern workmen's bath house was built to replace the existing facility which was constructed in the 1930s. The new 1950s bath house was demolished when the pit closed but the old 1930s structure still stands and contains features that are unique making it a Grade Two listed building.

Lisle Downie, the Ellington Colliery horsekeeper was Anthony Eden's batman during the 1914-18 war. Thirty eight years later it was arranged for the two to meet up again when the then Prime Minister visited Lynemouth Colliery. What was a scheduled five minute meeting grew to a 45 minute chat about old times. Mr Eden on his departure gave Lisle the yard stick he had been presented with on his visit.

Prime Minister Anthony Eden paid a flying visit to the pit in 1956 to view the modernisation carried out on the surface and underground. Lynemouth went on to fulfill its potential by becoming a major coal producer until a disastrous underground fire in 1966. Anthony Eden is pictured on the left with Coal Board officials after his tour.

After the underground fire, the old shafts were filled with water and a new drift sunk to access the north side of the workings. Two new shafts were sunk and the old shafts and buildings demolished.

To access the north side workings by sinking a new drift beltway for transport of coal and men, meant crossing the River Lyne before going underground. This was done in 1967 and this picture shows the river now diverted to the left to allow construction work to progress.

The new Bewick Drift beltways for transport of coal and men from the pithead to the underground transfer point now complete, prior to adding the conveyor belts to the structure.

It was not long after the fire that men were recalled to the pit to resume working in the north side district which was unaffected by the fire and the flooded and sealed off south side workings. Ron Dickinson is at the head of this group of men heading for the pit baths after their shift underground. Lynemouth lad, Dave Hindmarsh, is fourth left and Tucker Ewart is far right of picture.

Clocking in before going underground with a time card and out again when the shift ended was the method of keeping check of hours the men worked. Here is a view of the new time hall used at the Bewick Drift head.

The new Bewick Drift transfer point loading coal onto the overland belt leading directly to the Lynemouth Colliery surface facilities. A larger quantity of coal was fed by connecting belts to the Alcan power station hoppers.

When the Ellington Combine closed in 2005 there was no need for the overland belt that once carried coals to Lynemouth washery plant and so, as the picture shows, it was systematically demolished in June 2005 along with all the Lynemouth surface buildings save for the Grade Two listed bath house.

Alcan

Trust in the future of the revamped Lynemouth Colliery and neighbour Ellington to produce enough coal to service a new power station and subsequently enough electricity to power an aluminium smelter was great news for the area's economy. The building of the new power station and aluminium smelter sites, along with a Port of Blyth complex, began in 1969.

With a great number of different union bodies involved with the construction and different wage structures implemented it was inevitable that trouble would not be long in rearing its ugly head. First a series of wildcat strikes which escalated as time went by and at times there were ugly scenes on the picket lines – just as happened later with the miners disputes of 1972 and 1984. However, after a troubled start the first aluminium was cast at the Lynemouth Smelter in 1972.

The present owner Rio Tinto Alcan is still the major industrial employer in the area but now the whole complex has been earmaked for sale. Adherence to government carbon emissions and falling aluminium prices in the global market are the reasons given by the company. A disastrous power failure on Tuesday, 14th December 2011 resulted in one of the smelters potlines being lost which cast huge doubts on the future of the smelter. Union officials and local MPs met with government officials in an attempt find a buyer. By mid January, MPs Ian Lavery and Ronnie Campbell along with Alcan Union officials met with a delegation from Rio Tinto Alcan including their chief executive who gave no indication to the Alcan delegation that there would be any change to their closure programme.

After retired workers were invited to a closure 'Open Day' in May 2012 the company then declared in July 2012 that a funding scheme to assist local organisations would be set up along with a website to monitor the decommissioning of the smelter plant over the coming years.

In December 2012 a press release stated that the garage repair building at the smelter would be taken over by a firm which would create 25 jobs. The same source also said that the taking over of the power station by a German company RWE, which may convert to use biomass fuel, was well under way.

In 2013 the whole of the Alcan Farms was purchased by the Crown Estates and then in March 2015 Harworth Estates, the trading arm of UK Coal, took ownership of the smelter complex.

The following nine photos show the construction of the smelter and power station in 1969/70.

One of the first tasks before construction of the smelter was to lay a surface water drain to the main Ashington to Lynemouth road which was completed by March 1969. Lynefield Farm on the left was once tenanted by the Yellowley family and recorded on old maps in the Woodhorn Parish. The Grange Farm seen among the trees at the rear was demolished when the smelter was complete. The 19th century main house was  left standing and became a conference centre for the Alcan employees but it too was razed to the ground in 2009.

A unique picture showing a supervisor inspecting the base and steelwork surround at the start of the building of the first of the potroom's eight giant chimneys.

The 4th August 1969 and the east end smelter potroom bases are under construction. In the background is Lynemouth Colliery with the two shaft towers, soon to be demolished, still standing at this time after the underground fire.

Work proceeds apace with the smelter potroom column bases now bedded down and the pot floor supports being installed in September 1969. Lynemouth village is visible middle right above the structure and Ellington Colliery in the centre.

A bird's eye view of the smelter and work in progress on the potroom roof and one of the eight chimneys. In the background work on the carbon plant is well underway as is the building of the central maintenance top left.

Inside 2A potroom – now under cover, contractors are working flat out on 24th November 1970 to lay the pot bases before the introduction of the line of pots from which molten aluminium would eventually be produced.

A rail link to the smelter from the Alcan complex at the Port of Blyth was essential for the transport of materials and the export of produce. A new track was laid from the existing Lynemouth Colliery railway at Woodhorn and a new bridge built which crossed the Woodhorn to Lynemouth road near Lynefield Farm. Here contractors are laying the track and bridge supports over the road in November 1970.

Right: Work on the power station complex began in early 1969 and construction of the giant chimney windshield in August. Foundations for all the station buildings are shown here being laid down by contractors.

Left: October and the chimney windshield grows ever higher with the skeletal structures of the pump house and other buildings now taking shape. Bottom left at the side of the chimney is Lynemouth Colliery battery with coal wagons.

This picture shows a group of French Canadians who were brought over from the Alcan smelter in Canada to oversee training and commission machinery in various departments until the local workforce proved capable of managing in what was a totally new environment.

The complete picture in 1980 with the old Woodhorn Grange Mansion House in the left foreground. Behind is the Alcan smelter, with the power station and chimney back right. Lynemouth Colliery is seen back left and shows the Bewick Drift belt as it rises above the Lynemouth to Cresswell road.

October 2011 and the construction of one of Scottish Powers' 13 gigantic wind turbines is well under way on land to the south and west of the Rio Tinto Alcan Aluminium smelter. Pictured behind there seems little hope now of saving the smelter and the jobs of over 500 local people employed there.

The interior of the potrooms at the open day in May 2012 shows ex-employees, the author and his son Neil, standing in front of service vehicles and the two lines of pots that ran the whole length of the potroom in which molten aluminium was produced.

The casting plant that produced the aluminium ingots from molten metal still had work to complete and would be the last department to close down. Pictured here at the open day are a group of casting plant employees.

May time and the turbines are in operation towering above the central maintenance and carbon plant on the left.

Remember the Days of the Old School Yard

Lynemouth Council School could not have had a worse start to its life, opening on the 3rd May 1926 – the very first day of the General Strike. Staff employed to receive the first influx of pupils were Headmaster George T. Herron, James Reekie, Jane Frears, Edith Foster, Edna Mitchell, Isabella Elliot, Edith Jacques and Ethel Trueman. The Attendance Officer was Mr Raisbeck.

School Management was initially overseen by local businessmen, dignitaries and Labour Party members with Ashington Coal Company Officials keeping a close eye on the project within their new model village. The Rev Moore and Mr John Charlton attended the opening.

School Managers and Governors: Reverend Moore, Mr Lawson, Mr John Charlton, Dr Tom Skene, Mr McGuire from Ellington pit union, Mr Holliday the pit manager and Mrs Medlen of the Labour Party.

During the seven month coal stoppage records show that some Lynemouth children did suffer during this period. Although mining families and friends set up a soup kitchen to ensure at least one substantial meal a day was taken, that all depended on what food was available and how generous local traders were. Reports show that the outdoor preparation of meals was often disrupted by weather conditions.

Regular checks were made on the state of the children's nutrition by Dr Shepherd of the County Schools Department and by 6th October malnutrition was evident in some of the youngsters while many of the children attended without proper clothing or shoes. There was no fuel delivery to the school for heating purposes and pupils were made to exercise to keep warm.

The effects of the 1926 strike were even more evident during November shortly before the coal dispute came to an end when only 319 children registered owing to bad weather and lack of clothing and shoes.

The makeshift soup kitchen erected by these Lynemouth men in 1926 on the Dene Bank opposite the school, using a tarpaulin strapped to wooden poles. Left to right standing include: Mr Simpson, Mr Bates, Mr Leary, Mr Douglas, Mr Johnson, Mr Gallon, Mr Hudson, Mr Cleverley. The men crouching at the front are: Mr Cochrane, Mr Finlay and Mr Crawford.

Parents and friends helping out at the soup kitchen with pails and pans at the ready waiting for the ingredients to cook before taking over to the school and serving out to the children. Only once during extreme weather did they fail to provide a hot meal for the children. The lady on the left is Mrs Gallon who lived in Dalton Avenue.

The after effects of the strike were to be realised by Lynemouth children during 1927 when outbreaks of Scarlet Fever, Measles, Ringworm, Influenza and Chicken Pox was rife in the village.

A respite for the schoolchildren came in 1928 when the Duke of York visited Lynemouth and the whole school was taken out to view proceedings as he was driven around the village and visited some of the miners' homes. However, a damming report by Robert Booth in 1929 suggested teaching standards and pupils' work was unsatisfactory with the pupils still without adequate clothing and footwear. There was now 76 houses unoccupied in Lynemouth as the Ashington Coal Company had delayed the sinking of Lynemouth Colliery until 1927 due to the coal stoppage and miners were not yet required for work.

Right: All of the main Ashington Coal Company Directors and officials were present for the visit of HRH the Duke of York to the model colliery village of Lynemouth in 1928. He arrived in a car with Director Jonathan Priestman and met Sir Leonard Milburn, J.J. Hall, Ridley Warham and J. Pumphrey before inspecting some of the workmen's homes.

On 11th May 1930 a new government scheme was set up to provide pure milk each day for schoolchildren. At Lynemouth 158 pupils were supplied on the first day.

By 1931 the empty houses in Lynemouth were now being filled and by 1933, owing to increasing numbers of pupils, two classes took lessons in Lynemouth Methodist Chapel.

Minnie Dunn's class of around 1930. She was one of the early teachers who taught here for many years. Only four names known and three of them boys who all went on to become electricians at Ellington Colliery. Back row fourth left is Jim Nicholson, first left second back row is teacher Minnie Dunn, fifth left is Alf Goodall, seventh is Ken Hanson.

A school concert played out on the green between the classrooms and the hall, circa 1936. Only one pupil is known – Margaret Simpson standing far right of picture.

Lynemouth School netball team, 1937. Back row: Mary Huntley, Vera Brown, Betty Spowart, Esther Oliver. Front row: Betty Moore, Iris Musgrove, L. Cram.

Evacuees

At the end of September 1939 Lynemouth Council School, as it was then known, received an influx of children from two Newcastle based Roman Catholic Schools. These youngsters included 120 war evacuees from St Columba's School, Wallsend and 53 from St Lawrence School in Byker. Both these schools were near to the Tyneside docks area which was a natural target for enemy aircraft during the Second World War.

Bussed out to be housed with mining families in little old Lynemouth would have been an exciting but strange experience for these 11-14 year old 'toonies'. Winnie Wynn (née Connell) from Wallsend was one of them and takes up the story:

'We travelled to Lynemouth by bus, it took us half the day then. Some of our teachers went with us to stay as we were Catholics and had to be taught in that way. My aunt was one of the teachers. My sister didn't come with us – she was sent out into the countryside. I stopped with an old couple, Mr and Mrs Morton, who lived in Ingleby Terrace. They were nice and had a son who lived opposite with his family.

'We went to school for half a day and the Lynemouth children the other half which worked well. On Sundays we attended mass at the Lynemouth Hotel along with the locals and the Priest came from St Columba's to conduct the service. The place stank of beer and cigarette smoke with beer glasses and ash trays still scattered around.

'I liked my time there walking in the Dene and the seashore was just down the road where we played. I can remember there were ponies in the field and I think they were from the pit next door. I only stayed for a short few months and some of us went back to Wallsend with some of our teachers.'

Left: Wyn Connell's class at St Columba's, Wallsend in 1939 shortly before these girls were evacuated to Lynemouth – as were many other schools, away from the dangers of war. Wyn is fourth left in the back row. A number of these youngsters have now passed away, but Wyn still sees some of her old classmates at church.

Lynemouth County Primary

After the Second World War and a change in the education system, the school now became known as a County Primary School still catering for youngsters from age five to fifteen unless fortunate enough to move on to Grammar School when passing the old 11plus examination. Some pupils who showed promise sat an examination at 13 years of age to progress to higher education.

Lynemouth School in the late 1940s through to the 60s was noted for winning the area's senior boys prestigious Gillespie Cricket Shield. During these golden years they had the honour of claiming the trophy three seasons in a row. This was no mean feat for a small school like Lynemouth. This is the school team of 1950 displaying the Gillespie Shield. Back row: Alfy Shepherd, Gordon Crawford, Neal Kelly, Rene Teasdale, Brian Anderson, sportsmaster Bob Youngs, Ron Cleverley. Front row: Jakey Turnbull, Don Liddell, Harry Shears, Bill Barrass, Alec Mitchell.

A Junior 3 class from 1951 when these young pupils were around 10 years old and prior to taking the Education Board's 11 plus examination. Includes – back row: Gordon Renwick, Stan Brewis, Robby Willis, D. Harrigan, George Heard, John Tuck. Second back row: Margaret Green, Ann Houlison, Mavis Hall, Alma Davison, Valerie Stewart, Olive Graham, Fern Marsh, Elizabeth Wilson. Third back row: Richard Crewe, John Rochester, Michael Brown, Denis Gray, Ray Hindmarsh, John Streener, Ted Cooper, Bill Gates. Front row: Lynn Lewins, Sheila Clark, Isobel Graham, Pat Proudlock, Joan Young, Amy Herron, Noreen Gillis.

Field study programmes were available to the County's schools at Ford Castle, home of the Joicey family that was leased to the Education Authorities for a peppercorn rent. Here are some of the Lynemouth party who attended a course there in 1957. Back row: Terry McSparron, third left Brian Reed, fifth left Billy Johnson. Second back row: Judith Crawford, Doreen Hanson, fifth Alfy Urban, sixth Derek Goodall, eighth George Railston. Third row: second left Margaret Henderson, Ada Robinson, Joyce Tweddle, far right Andrew Hyslop. Second row: Mr Cessford, third Malcolm Lane, eighth Valerie Taylor, Kathy Danford. Front row: Carol Rhodes, Mary Hogg, fourth Clive Davidson, Albert Willis.

Headmaster of Lynemouth School, Mr Graham, back right of picture, led a group of Lynemouth pupils at Ford in 1956 with many of them seen here in this group photo call.

Left: Lynemouth and Ellington girls with two other school friends pictured in the Morpeth Girls High School grounds in 1955 – all looking very smart in their High School outfits. Back row: Valerie Stewart, Pat Charlton, Joan Youngs, Brenda Wilkinson, Nancy Carruthers. Front row: Pat Proudlock, ? Sheila Appleby.

Right: Brownrigg Camp Boarding School at Bellingham in the rural west of the County attracted pupils from many schools around the area. For the Lynemouth party it would be the first time living away from the confines of a close-knit pit village. Shown here are the Lynemouth boys contingent in 1953. Back row: Ron Srachan, Billy Gray, Jacky Herron, Tom Charlton, Jack Patrick. Middle row: Brian Lonsdale, Brian Davidson. Front row: George Amos, Gerry McGee, Ron Nicholson.

Below: Survivors from this school 1955-56 soccer team will have reached their three score years and ten. Back row: Andrew Hyslop, George Railston, Arthur Hanson, Bill Taylor, Ken Redpath, Johny Graham. Front row: Denis Gray, Keith Taylor, Arthur Kidd, Billy Dent, Owen Taylor.

Music teacher Audrey Stimpson with a Senior 2 class of 1955. It was not uncommon to find over 40 pupils to teach in one class in those early years. Back row: Clive Davison, Tom Horn, Bob Cowans, Mick Wharton, Malcolm Lane, Andy Brotherton, Owen Taylor, Albert Willis, Noel Stafford, Keith Taylor, Fred Cairns, Tom Rose. Middle row: Bill Johnson, John Chatt, Shears, Terry McSparron, Brian Reed, Judith Crawford, Gladys Hume, George Mavin, Harry Charlton, John Agar, Trevor Graham, Rodney Fenwick. Front row: Ann Simpson, Kathy Danford, Valerie Taylor, Elizabeth Ferguson, Rita Down, Audrey Stimpson, Mary Henderson, Margaret Nicholson, Maureen Anderson, Sheila Clark, Mary Pollard.

Every year prior to the Christmas holidays, a school pantomime was acted out on the stage in the school hall. This one contains pupils from senior classes of 1956.

A late 1950s picture of the Lynemouth teaching staff taken in the boys playground in front of the seniors classrooms. Many of these teachers taught at the school for a number of years. Back row: Irene Johnston, Susan Porritt, Bob Blair, Bob Youngs, Bob Nicholson, Elsie Snowdon, Jen Richardson. Front row: Marjorie Neave, Joan Bird, Miss Rhodes, Mr Graham (Headmaster), Mrs Graham, Audrey Stimpson, Marina Coombs.

An early 1960s picture of Infants 4 class taken outside the wooden hut that doubled as a classroom and an art studio at that time. Back row: Alan Bell, John Bryan, James Gray, ? Pollard?, Ian Hedges, Denis Marriot, Eric Robinson, Robert Robertson, Ian Poxton, Denis Redhead, Thomas Mears, Gordon Bell, Derek Maclean. Middle row: Michael Leonard?, Lyn Foster, Christine Taylor, Doreen Nicholson, Sandra Tait, Joan Kidd, Margaret Neder, Valerie Proctor, Rosemary Barnes, Janet Gilespie, Jaqueline Graham, Terry Brown, Derek Waddell, John Fieldson. Front row: Delia Patterson, Margaret Wynn, Hilary Love, Sheila Beers, Sandra Harding, Valerie Nelson, Rosemary Willis, Christine Day, Judith Maconachie, Evelyn Kirby, Christine Thompson.

Signs of affluence here in the dress of these smart young pupils when many of their fathers would be in full employment at either of the two collieries of Lynemouth or Ellington in 1965.

Long serving teacher Noreen Nixon with her class of 1966.

There is a real clue looking at the dress code and hair styles of these Lynemouth teachers that this is a 1960s photo. Back row: ?, Miss Snowdon, Mrs Reid, Mr Rogers, Mrs Duxfield, Mrs Tubby, Mrs Richardson. Front row: Miss Neave, Mrs Nixon, Mr Perris, ?, Mrs Gustard.

Lynemouth First School

There were further changes in the County education system in the 1970s when pupils who attained the age of 10 were moved on to middle schools and from 13 years on to high schools; this saw Lynemouth now operating as a first school catering for pupils aged from five to 10 years old.

Save for inclement weather and pantomime snaps it was unusual to see a class photo taken inside the school buildings during the school's early years as this one is. The hall seen here was originally used for assembly, school dinners, games, pantomimes and scholarship examinations. Long serving local teacher Marjorie Neave is shown here with her class of 1970s infants in front of the hall stage.

Taken in the boys playground in the 1970s. Members of the Sweet, Lister, Lynn, Scott, Moody, Taylor and Spratt families are among these children seen posing with their teacher for a class picture.

Looking east to the sea in April 2005 and the old school dinner hall was demolished to make way for the preparation of a new outdoor multi-use sports arena or MUGA as it is now affectionately named.

William Leech Campus

In 2008 a drastic shake up in the area's education programme saw Lynemouth included in an academy system with involvement from the Church of England. That meant name changes to many local schools. The names given celebrate prominent North East people and of course the funding trusts set up in their name. In Lynemouth's case, the name chosen was in honour of the William Leech Foundation. A real plus side to the operation of the new school and its young pupils are the high-tech educational aids and the influence and involvement of a chaplain from the Church of England. This comes at a time when many local churches of all denominations are suffering from falling congregation numbers and ultimately loss of revenue to support them.

After the closure of Lynemouth St Aidan's Anglican Church on Sunday, 3rd November 2013, the school authorities gave permission for St Aidan's adherents to hold a weekly service in the school hall for one year to give the clergy time to organise other facilities.

Parish of Cresswell & Lynemouth

Farewell Service

with The Rt Revd Martin Wharton
Bishop of Newcastle
at the close of the St Aidan's church building

and then
Procession to the
William Leech Campus
Northumberland Church of England Academy

St Aidan's Church
West Market Street
Lynemouth

Sunday 3rd November
5 pm

41

Lynemouth Church and Parish Hall with the Vicarage behind, built by Ashington Coal Company in 1925 to serve the growing community of Lynemouth. During its 88 year existence there have been 16 curates in charge of St Aidan's.

The old school green was the site chosen to build a new campus. The old school at the rear remained intact and pupils were educated here until the new facility was open. This picture shows the school green being cleared ready for the laying of founds for the new campus.

Founds laid and construction work on the new school under way in 2010. This photo looking west also shows the caretaker's house back left which is the only building now standing from the original school complex.

A view through the perimeter railings of the new school construction looking east from Eden Terrace and Dalton Avenue towards the old Co-op buildings on West Market Street.

The main building of the new high-tech William Leech Campus now operational and serving the children of Lynemouth from Easter 2011. The residents of the Dalton Avenue council houses would now have no view towards the north looking over Lynemouth Dene and the sea beyond.

Prior to a school art exhibition organised by Primary Leader, Helen Sample. On the 11th January 2013 a time capsule was buried in the school grounds by head boy, Brandon Clough and head girl, Jade Hamilton with the assistance of the author. Inside the capsule were photos, stories, artefacts and two books on the history of Lynemouth and its old school, plus poems, uniforms and similar artefacts created by the pupils of the new William Leech Campus.

Left: After the ceremony a good turnout of parents, teachers, classroom assistants and members of the general public attended an exhibition of the children's artwork in the school hall.

Below: A photo shoot for teaching and auxiliary staff at the Campus in 2015 with long serving caretaker, Stef far right front of picture, outnumbered by the ladies.

Shortly after the new school opened at Easter 2011, work began to demolish the old school and landscape the area. This is a picture just prior to when the old school closed on 28th March 2011, showing the former girls playground and original infants classrooms.

Resigned to the history books, now the west end of the old school is systematically demolished and two JCBs begin to clear away the debris.

Behind the two JCBs, a third machine begins to demolish the old boys end of the school and is busy pulling down the head teacher's office.

Children's Gala

A Gala for Lynemouth children was held at the Welfare facilities on Park Road each year from 1924 and well attended by children and adults.

Lynemouth man, Jim Simpson of Eden Terrace, marshalls the line of youngsters from the school along Dalton Avenue and eventually to the Welfare.

Ellington Colliery Band at the Welfare Gala in the 1950s with Alan Little and Bill Thompson at the front watched by a group of supporters.

Enjoying the day are Bob Fender, on the left, and Len Noctor, holding the dog. The boys in front are Ken Hanson, on the left, and Barry Summers. Jean Swinburne and Irene Smail are seen at the rear with their purchase of hot dogs from the vendor's van.

Every year a Gala Queen and two attendants were chosen to represent Lynemouth School at the annual July fair. In 1950 it was the turn of Park Road girl, Joan Mclean, to hold the honour with attendants Jean Taylor, on the right, and Dorothy Strachan, on the left.

Still operating in 2015 and run by Audrey Turnbull and her dedicated committee, young children of Lynemouth are shown at the start of the popular sprint races.

Noah's Ark in Lynemouth

Way back in 1999, Lynemouth's only two registered childminders, Lindsay Lamb and Joanne Fairfax, saw the need for more childcare facilities in the village. There was no option available for many parents who wished to return to work or study after the birth of their children.

After proving their claim for facilities, studying for management qualifications, writing up a business plan and even working part time, their dream was finally realised after four years when funding from the European Development Fund and the Dfes totalled £504,437 and allowed them to secure a brand new purpose built children's nursery. Local funding bodies then weighed in with £8,200 to purchase new play equipment.

It was never all plain sailing and the girls faced many problems along the way. So its hats off to Lindsay, Joanne and their staff as Lynemouth had a much loved and used children's nursery, being the only one in the immediate area. Taking in children from as young as six weeks old and having fully trained staff to see to children's needs. Noah's Ark Day Nursery sadly had to close its doors in 2013 due to many reasons but full credit to the staff who realised their dream in these difficult financial times.

The old Lynemouth First School annexe building on the right and later Lynemouth Library was intended to be the nursery before a fire laid low those plans and funding sourced to build a new facility on the same site.

However, Lindsay pictured the old annexe in the shape of an ark, hence the name of the new nursery.

Lindsay and Joanne in the centre of picture with friends and children standing in front of the new nursery facility now well under way to completion.

Opening day and ready for occupying in September 2004. Lynemouth children's new nursery, in a quiet position opposite the church and standing high above the River Lyne and Chugdon Wood.

The opening ceremony of the Noah's Ark Nursery was held on the 1st September 2004. Ex-Newcastle United star, Peter Beardsley, more attuned to cutting through opponent's defences, is seen here with Joanne and Lindsay before cutting the ribbon to declare the nursery open.

Various local organisations weighed in with funding for all the childcare equipment needed for the inside of the nursery and the outdoor play area. One of these funders was Alcan UK who sent along representative John McCabe to see how their input had helped the new facility. He is shown here with Joanne and Lindsay and some of the nursery children.

Lynemouth & District Social Club

It was no mean feat by a handful of Lynemouth men who were involved in setting up the first social club in 1924. The early houses in the most up to date model mining village in the country built from 1921 were not tenanted until 1922. It was men from the early residents of Chester Square, Boland Road, Dalton Avenue, Eden Terrace along with a small number of Ellington Colliery men who were determined that a social outlet would be available to the growing community.

There were no shops, school, social recreational or transport services until 1925 and this meant a journey by shanks's pony to Ellington, Newbiggin or Ashington. Inspired by the growth and success of the social clubs in Ashington and local mining villages, a group of men met up and formed a committee headed by secretary, Bill Little, and chairman, Jack Maguire. They canvassed for 10 shilling shares and for many men this meant paying in instalments, but eventually the money was raised to purchase a plot of land from the sale of the Cresswell Estate.

It was the Ellington Branch of the Miners' Union who first acquired the plot which they sold to the Social Club Committee while retaining an option on 20 yards of footage to the north with a view to building a Miners' Union Hall.

Fortune was to smile on the Lynemouth men when Stakeford Social Club moved into a new brick building and sold their old ex-army hut to them allowing them a year in which to pay for the hut. Carted back to Lynemouth in triumph, the hut was erected on pre-arranged foundations laid down by the men themselves.

The new club was primitive to say the least as there was no water, electric or fuel

Long serving committee men when the club was thriving as the area's most popular social attraction in the 1960s. Back row: J. Laidler, J. Sandgren, S. Redshaw, J. Ross, T. Crawford, T. Scott, C. Sweet. Front row: J. Rirby, C. Taylor, W. Crawford (treasurer), R. Holmes (president), J. Huntley (secretary), J. Jenkins.

source. There were two rooms, a bar and a concert end and only one stove that glowed white hot in the centre of the bar room. The clubmen bought a Donkey Engine and generated electricity, bored for a water source and the doorkeeper collected coals spilled on the road nearby. It may have been primitive but it was their club and it was up and running. The opening in November 1924 was celebrated with the sound of bottle tops popping as the draught beer had not been delivered on time.

The little club was thriving and affiliated to the CIU in February 1926, and then along came the 1926 strike and the depression years. Owing £600 to creditors with a bank overdraft of £100, only skilful handling of finances kept the club above water. In 1933 a new single storey brick building to the north west and a separate steward's cottage were built and rose quickly like a phoenix from the ashes. Named as Lynemouth & District Social Club, it was built by Mr Telford of Widdrington and opened by Lynemouth doctor, Tom Skene. Membership grew as Ellington Colliery expanded, employing more men and the new pit at Lynemouth attracted many mining families into Lynemouth village. In the 1960s it boasted a new lounge and concert room which compared favourably with any social outlet on the club circuit. The slow rundown of the club began after a licqour license was granted to Lynemouth Institute in 1968 which took away trade from the club which was sited midway between the villages of Ellington and Lynemouth and more difficult to access. With the membership declining, the closure of Lynemouth Colliery in 1983 followed by Ellington's closure under British Coal in 1994, it was obvious that the club was losing the battle to maintain those early miners' dreams of a thriving social club. Run for a short period as a private concern, there was no going back to the good old days and, like many other social outlets in coalfields all over Britain, the doors were finally shut in 1996.

Old pictures of the committee, mining and local scenes along with club records I rescued are now housed in Woodhorn County Archives. The main building and the cottage stood empty for some time and in need of urgent repair before being sold off and renovated by private owners.

The social club members and their kin, especially prior to and after the Second World War, were well known for their ability to compete successfully at games and events both inside and outside the club premises. During this period a team of hot shot darters and Lynemouth footballers created two separate pieces of history.

In 1946 a display of sporting trophies was exhibited behind the club bar that is unique and can never be repeated again. On show were the Northumberland Football Senior Cup, the Ashington Hospital Cup, Blyth Knight Memorial Cup and the Booth Cup – all won by Lynemouth Welfare Football Club. Also displayed was the Northumberland Junior Cup won by the Lynemouth Welfare Junior team. Lastly was the Northern CIU Darts Trophy won by the club team.

In 1950 behind the club bar stood two CIU darts trophies one of which the darts team had won outright in a rather strange yet determined fashion that had a fairytale ending. To win the trophy outright, it had to have been won five years in succession. Lynemouth won it two years before the war and then the competition was suspended until hostilities ended. After the war they then went on to win it three times in succession and claimed the trophy as their own property. There was much debating in CIU circles and arguments raged as to the validity of the Lynemouth claim. At a meeting of the CIU executive at Saltburn the panel ruled that because the five Lynemouth Club victories had not been in consecutive years owing to the intervention of war then the trophy had not been won outright. This did not faze the Lynemouth hot shots who promply went on to win it again and again and make five victories in consecutive years and claim the trophy outright.

The club darts team shortly after the war years. Left to right: Bill Foster, Bill Nicholson, Herbert Fieldson, Isaac Nicholson, Jim Ross, Bob Nicholson, Jacky Gowland, George Reilly, R. Ogilvie, Alex Nicholson, Jim Laidler, unknown, Jack Huntley (club secretary).

Many of the club committee in the early years were dyed in the wool Miners' Union members and eventually, as the club prospered, provision was made financially and socially to sustain the older retiring members and their spouses.

After the Second World War the old members would receive in each year £1 spending money, a tea and a concert. The ladies received a packet of tea and the men tobacco and cigarettes. At the miners' holidays and again at Christmas they were given £1. For those members who were working but on the sick for ten consecutive weeks, £5 was given in benefit. Lynemouth Club was certainly looking after its own.

Above: Old members of the club and their spouses are pictured here enjoying the benefits provided by the committee and members at a tea and concert in 1950.

This was the view outside Lynemouth Social Club in 1983 looking east down Lynemouth Road. The water tower, constructed in 1920 opposite what is now Charlton's caravan storage site, originally supplied water to the new village of Lynemouth built from 1921. The club car park area on the left is now the grounds of a private house.

Above: People turned out to stand in the club car park and watch as a piece of the area's history came crashing to the ground.

Left: After demolition in 1984, the tower lost its legs but the top fell still intact. A group of four men discuss the next move with Ellington Colliery Head Mechanical Engineer Matty Richardson (far right).

People and Places

Right: An early bus with staff and passengers outside the West End Co-op. Bill Kidd and Joe Swinhoe are two Lynemouth men sitting in centre of picture. All buses in the early 1920s that ran from Ashington to Lynemouth came by Ellington. The road by Woodhorn was not then made up

Above: James Bower of Bedlington was an early 20th century entrepreneur much in the same mould as today's Sir John Hall of Metro Centre fame. James, who set up an engineering and general dealer business in Bedlington Market Place, soon realised the potential of local transport and ran a bus service around the area employing family and local people. His daughter, Annie, married Ellington miner Jim Simpson of Eden Terrace, Lynemouth. Here is Jim, top left, inside the Bower Coach with Annie and baby Margaret below, with other members of the family.

Left: A 1928 picture of the conductress on the Lynemouth bus all neatly turned out and ready to collect fares with her ticket machine and money bag at the ready.

Lynemouth, as expected with its mining connections, had a strong affiliation to the Labour Party. These ladies, outside Mrs Medlen's home at 11 Eden Terrace in 1926, were the first female Labour Party members in the village and gave great support to the miners during the 1926 stoppage and the depression years of the 1930s. Back

row: Mrs Sunby, Mrs Tindall, Mrs Finlay, Mrs Routledge, Mrs Summers. Front row: Mrs Lawson, Mrs McGuire, Mrs Medlen, unknown, Mrs Sweet.

Mary Twizell from Newbiggin was a familiar figure around the Lynemouth streets hawking her seafare to the colliery folk. With a creel on her back and pushing a handcart with on board scales, it was no easy task. This photo, taken between Neville Square and Park Road, shows Mary weighing out a portion of fish to a Lynemouth lady in the 1960s.

Ernie Shears suffered severe facial injuries during the Great War and later came home to live in Lynemouth. Ernie was well known in the village doing odd jobs with his horse and cart. He also owned a brake which he used to transport folk on outings to the local beaches at Sandy Bay and Cresswell. This picture was taken from opposite Park Road in 1930 where Queen Street now stands.

With easy access to woods and fields new young miners to the village found the ideal places to walk and train their dogs while local farms encouraged men to bring along their terrier dogs to hunt rats at harvest time. Here four of the terrier brigade are pictured with their canines by the River Lyne in Ellington Dene. Left to right: Jack Weddell, Dick Simpson, Bill Waddell, unknown.

Before River View was built Prefabs were erected on that site in 1947 to accommodate the influx of miners arriving in the area to work at Ellington and Lynemouth Collieries. Bill Stewart was one of those men seen here at his home at no 6 having a natter with a neighbour.

The male members of the Graham family were originally from Longtown before working at pits in the Haltwhistle area, then moving to the Nottinghamshire coalfield after the South Tyne Colliery closed down. On returning to Haltwhistle the men were headhunted by Lynemouth Pit manager Mr Gibson to work at the newly opened pit at Lynemouth in 1937. Here are the Graham men and their wives settled at Lynemouth in the 1950s.

Many of the 1950s Darby and Joan Choir were among the original residents of Lynemouth and won a number of singing competitions throughout the years they were in operation. Here they are displaying some of their silverware in front of St Aidan's Church Hall.

It was common practice in pit villages like Lynemouth to find families taking their annual holidays together at places like Scarborough or Blackpool. This is one such occasion in the summer of 1950 when members of the Dalton Avenue and Eden Terrace clans invaded Blackpool. The families included are: Green, Shears, Cleverley, Scott, Cooper, Nicholson, Leader, Johnstone and the Hansons.

Lynemouth Hotel

Lynemouth Hotel. 8541.

Formerly Lynemouth Inn, this pre-Second World War postcard shows the fine mock Tudor style building now trading as a hotel without public residential facilities. Two main doorways are seen at the front with flower beds surrounding the front and sides.

The Coronation of Queen Elizabeth II in 1953 was held on a wet and windy day in June. Schoolchildren were escorted to the 'Gaiety' Picture House at Lynemouth Institute to see the event on the big cinema screen. It was a washout for street parties but Lynemouth Hotel became the venue for a tea party celebration for children from the area around the streets close to the hotel. Mrs Thornton and Mrs Templey, front of picture, are the ladies making tea with Mrs Gargett to the left and Mrs Harding. These ladies all lived in Matlock Square. Nellie Chapman is far right and many of the other children and parents came from Neville Square, Oakland Terrace, Bridge Road and Kingsley Road.

Lynemouth social establishments soon organised flower and vegetable shows from the 1920s. Annie Jewitt's husband, Bill was a keen exhibitor in the leek class and Annie is seen holding two of Bill's well grown specimens which took first prize at Lynemouth Hotel in 1973.

Lynemouth – In Lyne Resource Centre

Formerly the Lynemouth Inn and later Hotel, the Resource Centre was opened in 2000 to serve the immediate communities. It boasts a popular café, library, IT facilities, local organisation meeting rooms and a thriving chocolate company formed in 2009 – named Kenspeckle. This name is taken from old Northumbrian and means 'distinctive'. The outlet, which is growing apace, is already selling its popular products to local outlets, markets and to Selfridges of London.

In July 2013, the Resource Centre Community Trust was awarded a grant of £53,000. This came from a legacy fund from the nearby Rio Tinto Alcan Aluminium Smelter which closed with the loss of 500 jobs. The grant helped the business grow, win new orders and create employment in the village.

Kenspeckle benefited by acquiring new equipment to its Resource Centre based factory and recruited four more employees. The café was also rewarded with two existing jobs being safeguarded and new equipment purchased to promote the popular sales of jams and preservatives. A third ambitious scheme to benefit is a project named Weave headed by local lady Ann Kidd aimed at small independent textile designers and manufacturers where self-employed people can produce and market their own creations at the Centre. By 2015, Weave has progressed rapidly and trades with the famous toy store Hamley's – making staff outfits in the style of toy soldiers, racing outfits and doll like dresses for Hamley's branches across the UK, Europe, the Middle East, Asia and Russia.

Word has spread rapidly concerning the former pit villages 'Jewel in the Crown' Resource Centre and it was given a royal seal of approval when the Earl of Wessex visited on the 1st May 2015.

Rio Tinto's Joanne Hannay centre, pictured with left to right: Lynemouth Resource Centre's 'Choclatier' Dawn Watts, Community Trust Chairman Bill Tarbit, Centre Manager Andrew Gooding and Centre Assistant Melanie Dennis after the award ceremony at Lynemouth.

The Earl of Wessex arrives at the Centre and is soon chatting to the young pupils of Lynemouth's William Leech Campus First School, who have turned out in numbers to greet him.

Trust Chairman Bill Tarbit welcomes and introduces the Earl to guests before escorting him to view the many facilities at the progressive Lynemouth Centre.

Above: A proud day for café assistant Mandy York Jackson as she poses with the Earl in one of the doll like dresses produced for Hamley's by Ann Kidd in the Centre's textile room.

Right: Much impressed with the Centre's achievements the Earl speaks to locals before taking his leave and heading off to a further engagement in the area

Sport

The Littles of Lynemouth

Lynemouth through the years has produced a fair compliment of sporting heroes. Yet little is known today by new residents in the village of Alan and Ella Little's footballing family. Ellington Colliery electrician and brass bandsman Alan and wife Ella (née Foster) produced three sons, Brian and Alan who went on to play soccer at a high standard and young Ken who starred at local league level

The reason so many people are not aware of the Little family connection to Lynemouth is simply because Alan and Ella moved out of the district in the 1960s when the boys were young.

Dad, Alan of Henley Square, was something of a musical whiz kid when he played in Ellington Colliery Band. As well as being a super cornet player he was also a master of the flugal horn. Headhunted by Horden Colliery band in Durham, they offered him a job at the local pit and the added bonus of a key to the door of a colliery house in which to raise a growing family. Sadly, Alan died at his home in Peterlee in 2011 after a long musical career playing and conducting for Horden, Blackhall and Hartlepool bands.

Brian and young Alan as schoolboys showed outstanding ability, attracting the attention of football league scouts. They signed up for Aston Villa and played in their successful youth team of the late 1960s and early 70s. Brian's career rocketed and he progressed rapidly through the ranks until he was a regular first team member alongside players like Andy Gray and John Gidman. The highlight of his playing career was when he was selected for the full England squad.

The successful Aston Villa youth team with the two Little brothers firmly established in the side. Defender Alan is third left in the back row and forward Brian sitting third right in the front. Brian is now Director of Football for Jersey.

A bad injury would see Brian ending his playing days with Villa, the only club he had ever turned out for. Turning to coaching and management, he quickly made his mark with spells at Middlesbrough, Wolves, Darlington, Leicester, Aston Villa, Stoke, West Bromwich Albion, Hull, Tranmere, Wrexham and Gainsborough while finding time to make his comments as a TV pundit which he still does today.

Brother Alan's career after leaving Villa saw him playing for Southend, Doncaster, Halifax, Hartlepool and York where he ended his playing days and had a spell as manager there before leaving the soccer scene.

Stuart (Shack) Chapman

Stuart Chapman was born at number 5 Neville Square, Lynemouth in 1951, just a stone's throw away from the Welfare Park. This is where he spent much of his leisure time, honing his skills as a promising young footballer.

In 1966 while Bobby and Jackie Charlton were helping England win the World Cup Stuart left school and signed up for Sir Stan Matthews who was then manager of Port Vale.

Stuart was known as Shack because of his ball playing skills similar to his idol Len Shackleton of Sunderland. He had played for Newbiggin School, East Northumberland and the North of England School Boys before moving to Vale and made his debut for them at only fifteen years of age against Lincoln in the Fourth Division. After four seasons there he moved to Stafford Rangers in 1970 and stayed for 14 years until 1984 being given a testimonial match against West Brom in November 1978. Moving to Macclesfield for one season, Stuart 'Shack' Chapman played out his long career in professional football in 1985. Stuart lives in the Midlands but still comes home to visit.

Sir Stanley Matthews, Port Vale manager on the left, welcomes Stuart and a group of promising young footballers from around the country to the club facilities.

Stuart Chapman went onto play for Stafford Rangers in the 1970s and 80s.

Wor Jackie

Lynemouth ladies played charity football matches well into the 1950s. This snap shows them before a match with Ashington ladies, being given some coaching from Ashington and Newcastle United's famous footballing hero Jackie Milburn.

Lynemouth Junior football teams were formidable opponents and saw much success in league and cup competitions. Here the 1953 team are shown prior to one of their league games. Back row: Referee, Jacky Hindmarsh, Jim Armstrong, Tommy Orr, Jacky Herron, Bob Strachan, Stan Bowey, Jim Stephens (Trainer). Front row: Ray Grey, Billy Gray, Dodds, Andy Johnson, Dave Wrightson.

John George Graham of Lynemouth kept up the family tradition of Cumberland Wrestling and won many competitions. This photo shows John being presented with the winners' cup in his weight category by the lady of the manor.

Champion of Champions is difficult to attain but John wears the belt to prove it and grandson, John George, retains the belt with pride.

The Lynemouth Lip

Sid Waddell, alias the Lynemouth Lip owing to his flowery style of TV darts commentaries, spent much of his boyhood years in Lynemouth his 'emotional home'. Son of miner Bob and Martha Waddell of Dalton Avenue, Sid, a fanatical Newcastle United fan, was an exceptional scholar and athlete. At King Edward Grammar School, Morpeth he played rugby for the school and received a number of County caps as well as winning many awards on the track as a sprinter. He left school with ten O levels and three A levels and a scholarship to St John's College, Cambridge.

Injury curtailed his outdoor sporting pursuits but he soon arranged the first inter collegiate darts tournaments and tried to get the game the same 'blue' status as other outdoor college sports. The rest is history as they say and after a successful career in TV writing and production, Sid became one of the most easily recognised voices in sport.

He was even named in the top ten of famous Northumbrians beating the likes of suffragette Emily Davison and footballer Bobby Charlton.

Sid wrote two books in his later years, the first 'Bellys And Bullseyes' concerned his life in darts and the second 'The Road Back Home' of his early life in a pit village.

Sid died at his home in Leeds in August 2012. What would have pleased him was the fact that the World Darts trophy has now been named the Sid Waddell Trophy.

Sid wearing his Magpies' strip and holding the Northumberland flag of gold and red in 2005.

Boxing

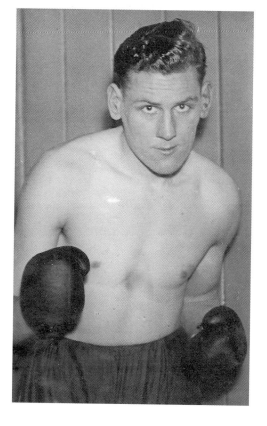

The Lister family lived in the end house next to us in Dalton Avenue. Ivan and Keith were around the same age as my brother and I. The Lister lads had two pairs of boxing gloves handed down from Uncle Harry and these were soon put to good use. We would spar in the backyard imagining we were world champs, wearing the great Harry Lister's gloves. However, this was not as easy as it might seem. Old Tom Lister was a great one for netting rabbits and there was always nets and rabbits hanging from a line across the yard. It was bad enough trying to dodge punches without the added hazard of avoiding skinned rabbits swinging on the line. The Lister lads had a horse and cart and pulled sea coal off the beach, then one day Tom bought a mule from Eddie Hanson and it was stronger than any horse and lived to a ripe old age.

Left: Heavyweight boxer Harry Lister at 21 was Britain's most promising young prospect. At 6 ft 2$\frac{1}{2}$ inches tall and weighing 14$\frac{1}{2}$ stone, he had 56 contests during his career, winning 53 of these.

61

Serving the Community

Lynemouth has had a number of residents over the years who have gone on to take prominent positions in society. One of these was a lady, Sarah Cowey, a JP who was a co-founder of the Lynemouth Branch of the Co-operative Women's Guild. In 1975 she became National President of that organisation.

It was 1978 when Lynemouth Co-operative Women's Guild celebrated its 25th anniversary. Here are officers and members at the event.

Right from the early years there were organisations set up in Lynemouth to cater for the needs of people both young and old. This was encouraged by the Ashington Coal Company who built the village. Their thoughts were that a contented workforce brings better results. This group contains some family members of the Lynemouth folk from the 1960s – Hall, Mclean, Fairfax, Kennedy, Strachan, Gordon, Taylor, Gray and others.

Sunday, 22nd May 2005 saw a memorable occasion when Lynemouth man, Councillor Milburn Douglas, attended a service of dedication at St Aidan's Church to welcome him home as the elected Mayor of Castle Morpeth. A parade of dignitaries, locals and other organisations headed by Morpeth Pipe Band marched from Park Road to the church for the ceremony. Behind the contingent, to the right, is Park View sheltered accommodation and left of that near the tree is where the Lynemouth Pit manager's house once stood.

Dougy, as he is affectionately known, being received into the church flanked by standard bearers. Chugdon Wood is seen in the background and the newly built Noah's Ark Nursery building is on the left of picture.

Lynemouth scouts and cubs were among those groups attending and some are shown here, marshalled by leader, John Harrison, at the rear as the parade heads back from the church along West Market Street.

After the ceremony, the mayor stands outside Lynemouth Resource Centre flanked by Anglican Minister Father Alan Simpson and councillors ready to salute the parade as they march past.

When Kathleen Holdroyd was asked to start up a dance school for the children of Lynemouth, little did she envisage that she would still be providing an educational and social outlet for the youngsters some 30 years on. Lynemouth Institute provided the facilities and the dancers have raised thousands of pounds over the years for charity. Kathleen is seen back, second left, next to Michael Douglas of Beaconsfield Operatic Society at the dance school's awards ceremony.

The demolition of the old Lynemouth Scouts' hut began in September 2003. This had been the headquarters of the cubs and scouts for 50 years as well as providing the village with extra community activities. John Harrison, the 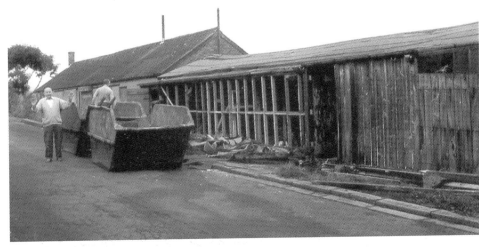 troop leader, is seen at the rear organising the project. The brick building behind was the Ashington Coal Company depot for the colliery masons and built at the time the first colliery houses were occupied in Lynemouth.

I remember when the scouts' hut was erected. I was a boy scout way back in the 1950s when our troop dismantled an ex-Second World War army hut at Widdrington and brought the prize back to Lynemouth on the back of a lorry. It took a whole day to dismantle and much longer to erect. An extension was added later to cater for more facilities. Tom Rankin, Ken Paynter and Bob Batey were the scout leaders at that time.

Lynemouth Primitive Methodist Chapel

Right: Lynemouth Primitive Methodist Chapel was opened for worship on 21st August 1927 by Lady Runciman and a tea was held in the Lynemouth Church Hall, where the guest of honour was Lord Runciman. He is seen here, sitting in the centre of the front row with Ashington Coal Company director, Francis Priestman and Methodist circuit officials.

Below: The first Lynemouth Methodist Chapel male members and officials who attended the opening ceremony and the tea pictured outside Lynemouth St Aidan's Vicarage.

Early lady members, Sunday School teachers and girls in the chapel gardens Included at the back are: Mrs Crackett, Mrs Armstrong, Mrs Taylor, Mrs Gallon, Miss Foster, Mrs Lane. Among the girls are: Cynthia Armstrong, Margaret Scott, Margaret Yole,

When Lynemouth Primitive Chapel opened in August 1927, the management committee soon became active with a programme geared towards encouraging young people into its fold. Sunday School, Rechabite meetings and pierots were just some of those groups that did exactly that. The

pierots here are some of the younger element at that time. Back row: T. McGeorge, E. Freeman, W. Barrons, W. Moody, R. Chatt, M. Tait, J. Gargett. Front row: J. Barker, W. McGeorge, E. Foster. J. Wilson.

Harrison (Sonny) Armstrong organised a lifeboys section at the chapel after the Second World War which proved popular with local youngsters and continued until the 1960s. Back row: John Lewins, John Taylor, Colin Birch, Eddy Rhodes, Billy Gray, Brian Freeman. Front row: Ezzy Mannion, George Clark, Clarry Green, Colin Farrier, Owen Taylor, Bill Chatt, George Heard, Alan Dickinson, Neil Taylor.

After almost 83 years of worship, Lynemouth Primitive Methodist Chapel closed for Church services on 8th June 2010. With one regular member and a handful of Day Centre worshippers, the clergy decided that the minister could be better used elsewhere on the circuit. On the right of photo Belle Reynolds, last surviving member shows her sadness at the closure. Joan Brodie (Cooper), whose mother was an original member, chats to Minister Barry Welsh.

Four ladies, all with chapel connections from the old days, stand in front of the Lectern. Left to right: Joan Brodie (Cooper), Olive Lemin (McGee,) Maisie Cuthbertson (Tait) and Jean Morris (Taylor).

Well on the way to healthy ways

Lynemouth doctors surgery was sited on Albion Terrace for some 78 years before a much needed high-tech building was erected at the west end of the village in 2003 to serve the surrounding communities. Looking a little run down, the old place has now been updated and used as a private dwelling.

The new premises at Lynemouth with much improved facilities just before completion in 2003. Now a part of the Wellway Trust, which includes surgeries at Morpeth, Pegswood and Newbiggin.

Dr Alistair Blair welcomes the Health Minister, the Right Honourable Jane Kennedy, to the official opening ceremony of the new Lynemouth Surgery in 2005 and introduces her to Councillor Milburn Douglas and his wife Ann.

Healthcare has moved on since the early years of having one doctor in the village. It is now possible in 2015 to telephone the surgery and see a doctor on the same day. Sometimes you may even be diagnosed and treated over the phone without ever being seen – 'talk about whizzkids'.

Introductions all round as the reception staff on duty gather to meet the minister and give their views on the facilities.

Above: A gift of flowers for the minister in the company of Dr Blair and long time Lynemouth residents, Bob Lamb and Gillian Thompson.

Left: Dr Blair and the health minister with most of the surgery staff on duty that day outside the new high tech building on Albion Terrace, built on the site of Lynemouth's old West Bridge.

Changing Face
A collage of the old and the new

Lynemouth faced many problems when the coal trains no longer ran through the village after the new Bewick Drift was built in 1968 and Ellington Colliery coal was fed direct underground into this new facility at Lynemouth. Eventually the line between the two collieries was used as wagon storage only and by the 1980s was not needed at all. This was the start of a major revamp of the area by the County Council which saw the railway lines removed in 1986 and the viaduct filled in while the West Bridge was demolished in 1992 and a new road link connected the houses at the north and south side of the village.

Right: An aerial view of Lynemouth in 1990 shows the changes that could be made to improve the village layout. The perfect oval of the Welfare cricket field laid out in 1925 by Ashington Coal Company can be seen top right of photo.

1986 shortly before the railway lines were lifted in the viaduct which curved around to the East Bridge between Albion Terrace on the left and Ingleby and Oakland Terrace to the right. The old doctor's surgery and Primitive Methodist Chapel are seen on the left of photo.

Looking east with the West Bridge still standing in 1988 and the railway lines to the right now lifted. To the left, the road over the bridge is shown. The road over the bridge and the bridge were demolished in 1992. This is where the new doctor's surgery was built.

A new footbridge over the railway lines was built in the centre of the village in 1969 to allow villagers on the south side easier access to Post Office and newsagents and the north side residents a walkway to the Welfare and allotments. This facility was taken down after the railway area was landscaped.

Built in 1925 by Ashington Coal Company to connect the people and services on either side of the road and railway in their new model village, the West Bridge was quickly demolished in 1992.

After the demolition, a peaceful scene in 1993 with the bridge now gone and a new made up road now linking the local folk to all amenities.

Looking towards the East Bridge in the viaduct and a Lynemouth Colliery diesel engine is seen hauling a set of wagons along the tracks for storage in the early 1980s. Alcan power station chimney built from 1969 is shown at the rear and the Bewick Drift beltway behind the bridge.

Changes in 1986 when the rail tracks were lifted down the whole length of the Ellington to Lynemouth railway. Only the old rail sleepers lying in the Lynemouth viaduct, a testament to what had gone before.

After the changes there was no coal dust or tanky smoke so it was then decided to add a little colour to the scene when the Parish Council sited two flower filled coal tubs at the East Bridge, close to Lynemouth Institute.

Looking west and the transformation caught here in this picture of the grassed and landscaped area between Albion Terrace and Oakland Terrace.

A major clean up of the river bank on the north side of the village was undertaken in the 1990s. This area behind the Boland Road scouts' hut and garages had been used as a local rubbish tipping ground for many years.

Work in progress by a team headed by youth leader, Colin Robson, to provide a walkway access through the reed beds behind River View and close to the River Lyne. This area is always wet and a natural flood plain when the river is in spate. As a boy I remember this place as our winter skating rink.

The works now complete, giving more access for the public and a safe area for the local school to learn about nature. The Dene beyond the river was known as the Private Dene by the older generations of the village simply because until 1924 it was part of the Cresswell estate and then owned by Ashington Coal Company who employed a gamekeeper to manage it for shooting

parties. As a young lad I always knew it as Lynemouth Dene. Its official name, as depicted on old maps, is Chugdon Wood.

This is the area where my boyhood friends and I spent much of our leisure time. Fallen trees across the river gave access to the Dene and safaris through the woods could take us as far as Cresswell Home Farm, Windmill Hill and on to Cresswell. We built camps, climbed trees and learnt much about nature along the way. This is where my lifetime interest in natural history began. Here is a poem I wrote some time ago after an encounter with an otter by the River Lyne.

Otter by the River Lyne

In the quiet of the night
When a big moon
Silvered dark pools
Between Alder and Hazel banks
Cruised the master
Of every swim there is,
Web footed spirit of all things river
Soft splashes in a midnight pool.
Then again one day at noon
In the Autumn of that year
Fresh pelted dark eyed fen dog
Questioned my right to view,
Then weasled away to his lair
Just as if he had never been there.

Neil Taylor

The picture says Lynemouth Dene and although not strictly true it is not difficult to understand why this happened. This is the Lynemouth end of Ellington Dene in the early 1920s when the only road into Lynemouth from Ellington was by a ford across the River Lyne. The new model village houses of Ingleby Terrace, Fenham Road and the early Park Road area would only be some two hundred yards above the river and the east end of Ellington Dene. Many of the Lynemouth children made this their playground.

Lynemouth Dene

The Dene, Lynemouth.

Looking west towards Ellington in the late 1920s and a new footbridge now spans the River Lyne at the Lynemouth end of Ellington Dene with the ford no longer in use. This footbridge was then forever known as the First Bridge. The Second Bridge, also a footbridge, was sited at the Ellington end. The first ever bridge to cross the river was a makeshift affair sited down by the church to access Chugdon Wood on the Cresswell side of the river. This was always known to locals as the 'Shakey Bridge' and was not in existence after the Second World War.

October 2002 and, after heavy rain in the area, the First Bridge is almost awash with floodwater and captured on camera by local man Charlie Sweet.

The Great War

The expansive and secluded Lyneburn and Cresswell coastal areas were ideal for housing and training troops for combat during both world wars. There are reports of many different regiments about the area including the Fife and Forfars, Scottish Horse, Tyneside Irish and the Northern Cyclists.

Local man Kit Furness joined the war effort in 1914 with D Company of the Northern Cyclists Brigade attached to the Tyneside Irish. Kit went on to win the Military Medal when attached to the 1st Battalion Northumberland Fusiliers during the 1914-18 conflict. Cyclists were used for reconnaissance and to carry messages in the field.

Right: Kit Furness with his sturdy bike on patrol at Woodhorn during an exercise with the Northern Cyclists.

D Company of the Northern Cyclists Brigade pictured at Lyneburn in 1914 at the beginning of the Great War.

Fred Richard Harding

Fred was 24 years old and a member of the TA at the outbreak of the Great War and left coal mining to join up with the 7th Battalion Northumberland Fusiliers as a Quartermaster Colour Sergeant. He was camped at Buryport, South Wales before leaving for France with the British Expeditionary Force.

His full war service record is not known but he was awarded four campaign medals all of which are proudly kept by his grandchildren. After the war he kept his involvement with the TA at the Ashington Drill Hall and is recorded there as a sergeant in 1921. He and the Drill Hall Company Commander returned to France then visiting battle sites and gathering information.

He is later known to have worked at Lynemouth Colliery as a hewer and then a datal hand and lived at 3 Guilford Square, Lynemouth. It was at the pit where he had an accident and lost an eye before retiring and living in 9 Jubilee Cottages where he died in 1966. Amazing to think that those brave young men who worked down the mines went off to war and of those who survived, back to the pit to face even more danger.

Sergeant Fred Harding is pictured far right of group at the start of the Great War.

Colour Sergeant Fred Richard Harding with the boxing gloves in a light hearted moment at camp with the 7th Battalion Northumberland Fusiliers in 1914 before campaigning in France.

The Second World War

Lynemouth miners during the Second World War rallied round to join the Home Guard and many hair raising incidents occurred during exercises. Alan Simpson recalled when he was a member of the company's bomb squad and on exercise at Druridge Bay: 'We practised throwing hand grenades and one I threw failed to explode on the beach. Me and Sergeant Jim Fotheringham crawled under barbed wire with an apparatus to explode the device but as we did we heard a click and buried into the sand just ten yards away as the grenade blew and luckily we came away uninjured. Another instance was one day in the Private Dene when doing target practice and stray bullets whistled over our heads as we marched single file along the track.'

John Robinson kept a record of some of the events from 1939-45 and remembers a German Dornier aircraft shot down over Druridge Bay on 17th October 1939 and then a report of a German aircraft going down there on the 3rd February 1940. Cresswell Lifeboat was called out and found nothing but three German airmen were buried at East Chevington at this time. 1941 saw increased activity in the skies over the area and Lynemouth suffered bomb damage and incendiary bomb attacks in May and September. A German aircraft was shot down over Druridge Bay in May and there were no survivors while a bomb exploded near to Cresswell Radar site. In June 1943 a German bomber was salvaged from the sea off Lynemouth. The four German airmen are buried at East Chevington. In 1945, John, a keen chess player, remembers playing chess at Lynemouth Institute against POWs released from Cresswell Camp.

Alan Simpson of Lynemouth, at 18 years old, all kitted out in Home Guard uniform at the front door of the Simpson house in Guilford Square in 1940.

In March 2014, after stormy weather, a pill box was found uncovered just off the dunes in Lyne Bay. Built with concrete filled sandbags, it is thought to have been built in the Second World War and used by the military and the Home Guard.

Gerald Tait's Wartime Memories

Now living in New Zealand, Gerald was a young boy living in Lynemouth during the war and vividly recalls those years: 'At first I lived in West Market Street before our family moved into a new house in Bridge Road. It was late 1940 when a flight of German aircraft flew over the village and everyone rushed outside to see them dropping propaganda leaflets. That was the only time, until February 1941 when a parachute mine was dropped, that we ever thought much about the war. After the mine exploded it left a giant hole 27 feet deep and 44 foot wide and demolished houses with others damaged. Unfortunately one lady, Mrs Athey, was killed and there were many injured and homeless.

'For young folk it was a frightening yet exiting time and I had little sleep that night. Next day I was late for school and when I arrived there was no one there. I went back home not knowing the school had been damaged and classes were being held in the Church Hall.'

Right: The morning after scene at the third block in the odd numbered Dalton Avenue houses in February 1941 when a German aircraft dropped a landmine on Lynemouth village.

Dalton Avenue, Lynemouth. 13.

A view from the front of the same street of houses on the left now rebuilt in the late 1950s. The only difference is that when these houses were rebuilt the backs were of a different design to pre-war damage. The two streets of Boland Road houses can be seen in the background.

U-Boats and Banknotes

Money was literally changing hands like confetti at Lynemouth during the war years. Banknotes, thousands of them, washed up in wooden crates at Lyneburn. My brother-in-law Tom Morris still has his booty, kept for over 70 years and has given me some of the banknotes to corroborate the story. They were thought to have come from a ship leaving the Tyne which was attacked by a German U-Boat which was hiding in Newbiggin Bay and under orders to engage with shipping leaving the Tyne. This theory was supposedly confirmed by the U-Boat captain who visited Newbiggin after the hostilities. The notes, in thick bundles, were washed up along the east coast and those at Lynemouth showed the picture of the first Chinese Republic leader Sun Yat-sen and not Chiang Kai-Shek as previous reports suggested. Sadly, the notes were worthless to the countless Lynemouth residents who waded into the sea and hauled the crates ashore to spirit away back home. It may have been better if it had been crates of spirits

like in that old film 'Whiskey Galore', at least there may have been some profit to be had in hard times when folk were queuing at shops for certain food produce that was scarce during the years of the war.

Left: The front of a banknote washed up at Lyneburn over 70 years ago showing the image of the first Chinese Republic leader Sun Yat-sen.

Cresswell Radar Sites

Connie Groves from Lancashire is now well over 90 years old with a mind as clear as a bell. She recalls vividly her Second World War service as a young WAAF at various radar sites across the UK. But her time working at the Cresswell site in 1945 and billeted in Lynemouth was special to her and resulted in a lifetime friendship with one family. Connie takes up her story:

'When I first came to Lynemouth I had to report to the Miners' Institute who had kindly allowed the RAF use of a room where the duty WAAF was stationed and met newcomers, showed them to their billets and was on call for any enquiries. On some radar sites I had served at, we were often housed in Nissen huts or old wooden ones taken over for the war. To be in civvy billets at Lynemouth was like being at home and the best six months of my service life. Everyone was so kind and generous and consequently I have a sincere love of Geordies and will have till my dying day. My time at 46 Eden Terrace with Mr and Mrs Jim Simpson and daughter Margaret was truly wonderful. We kept in touch for 63 years until Margaret died in 2008 which surely is proof of the affection I held for them.

'The radar station where I worked was on the left hand side of the Lynemouth to Cresswell road close to Cresswell Home Farm and had a big radar mast which could be seen from Lynemouth. It was known as a CHL station which plotted low flying aircraft and shipping. The one on the right

Connie Groves is shown here as a 20 year old newly recruited WAAF at the beginning of the Second World War. She had no idea then that she would eventually end up being posted to Cresswell and be billeted with a coalmining family in Lynemouth.

near Snab Point I believe was a GCI unit. They were capable of communicating by R/T to pilots of our fighters sent to intercept hostile aircraft and giving our lads position of enemy aircraft. We plotted everything both hostile and friendly and all shipping. Aircraft plots were given by direct telephone to the RAF Area plotting room and shipping plots to the Royal Navy plotting room at Newcastle with all information in code.

'Radar was a new invention and very secret. We who worked on it were sworn to secrecy not to divulge information and it was forbidden to discuss anything to do with radar outside the operations block. There was another WAAF in the same billet as me at Lynemouth who worked at the Snab Point operations block and we never once spoke about the job either of us were doing.

'Talk about unsocial hours, well ours certainly was. We worked a three watch system through the 24 hours starting on Monday from 8 am until 1 pm then back at 11 pm working through the night until 8 am Tuesday, before sleep and back on watch at 6 pm until 11 pm and again from 8 am on the Wednesday until 1 pm after which we had 24 hours off. I remember one night coming out of the back door in Eden Terrace at 10.30 pm to go on night watch and a crowd of miners were standing talking in the back lane. One said as we passed 'Canny shift thi night hinnies'. They probably wondered what on earth we did but nobody ever quizzed us about our job.

'We RAF and WAAF were allowed to use the NAAFI at the army camp along the road near to Cresswell where there were goodies for sale such as sweets, chocs, ciggies and cakes so it was a popular place for us, as all things in civvy shops were rationed. When I left Lynemouth in 1945 it was a thriving community with the Institute and the hotel

The ops room of a GCI Unit which plotted aircraft and shipping while communicating by R/T to pilots of our fighter aircraft.

much used. The hotel had dances there on certain nights of the week but my love was ballroom dancing and Margaret and I used to go dancing at the Co-op Hall in Ashington when I was off duty and then came home on the pit tankie. The Institute had a picture hall and was very popular. It was a good place for local people to meet up and see the news films about the war and then watch the main feature which was far removed from any hostilities and brought a sense of normality to our lives. Of course there was a blackout during the war years and it meant walking home in the dark but I was used to all that.

'My last visit to the area was in the late 1980s when I came back to visit Margaret who was then married to Jimmy Jacques and to do a little touring around the county. I was amazed that where the lower site at Snab Point had been there was nothing to be seen. The guardroom, admin offices, cookhouse, men's billets, rifle range and the GCI operations block had disappeared and so had some of the land, probably due to coastal erosion. I hope these notes are of some use as a historical record and of part of my duties during the Second World War as a young WAAF and living with a homely family at Lynemouth while serving my country at the Cresswell Radar Site. They were wonderful times that I will never forget.'

The operations block of a CHL station. WRENS and WAAFS doing shipping. Two operators on cathode ray tubes and not allowed to work more than one hour on these. One operator is seen inserting plots on shipping map and one operator on aircraft map. One WREN and one WAAF are recording all plots.

Editor: A strange occurrence was reported in the local paper about a young RAF serviceman during the war years who was on duty late one night at the guardhouse entrance to the Snab Point radar site. The young man saw a light in the sky which came ever nearer and then seemed to hover above him until it blinded him. He fell unconscious and was later revived by other personnel. He never wavered from his story and no explanation as to what occurred that night was ever given.

Lynemouth Picture Hall the first phase of the Institute, where Connie reported for duty on her arrival in Lynemouth, doubled as a theatre and was known as the Gaiety. It could seat 500 people, had a stage and the cinema screen behind that. At the rear was an elevated cinema box with the latest type cine projectors. Later the seating was changed and plush seats replaced the old bench type arrangement. Now the Social Centre Hall, it once was home to the Ellington Colliery Banner which is now retained by Ellington union officials at their Hirst Welfare, Ashington office.

Above: A group of Lynemouth special constables at the end of the Second World War after a meeting at the Welfare Ground. Jim and Jack Simpson, second and third right in front row, were on duty the night the land mine exploded. They saw the mine being dropped then helped rescue their brother Will and his family from the wreckage of their home. Will, also a special constable, is second from left in the back row.

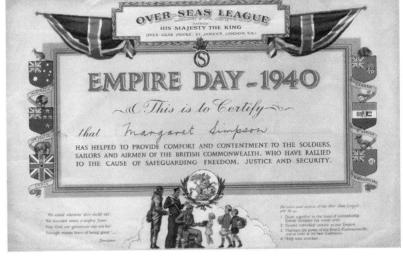

Above: Twelve year old Margaret Simpson was one of many children who supported the men fighting for the British Commonwealth during the Second World War. Here is one of her awards, a certificate from the Over-Seas League in 1940.

Lynemouth Welcome Home Fund

The Committee of the above Fund along with the Residents of Lynemouth hereby convey their thanks to

Dorothy Tilmouth.

for services rendered in H.M. Forces during the years 1939 to 1945.

This Memento, together with a small monetary gift, is an expression of our appreciation and gratitude for services in the cause of Freedom.

Mrs. G. D. GORDON, G. H. PROCTOR, W. REED,
Secretary. Chairman Treasurer,

Left: Lynemouth girl, Doris Tilmouth who later married Norman Teasdale, joined the war effort and was attached to the Royal Artillery serving at gun battery units up and down the country including the station at Blyth Links. Doris, who saw much devestation in London when stationed at Wandsworth, was kindly acknowledged for her efforts by the village Welcome Home Fund Committee on behalf of the village residents.

Norman Teasdale worked at Lynemouth Colliery and played in Ellington Band before enlisting in the army at the beginning of the Second World War. After training he was seconded into D troop No 12 Commando spending all of the war years fighting in Burma. Norman cuts a fine figure of a man in his unit outfit.

Back home to Jersey Square and to work at Lynemouth Colliery, Norman, seen here second left of bandsmen, soon returned to his band which was proving to be very successful at local and regional competitions.

Matty Willis

Lynemouth man Matty was 20 years old when he left Ellington Colliery to join the Northumberland Hussars Yeomanry in 1939. It was 1941 when the regiment were sent to Egypt and then on to Greece. His battery was then sent to the north of the country, travelling in freezing conditions over mountainous terrain with hairpin bends, tiny bridges and deep ravines. There were many accidents and injuries and in one of these Matty suffered a broken leg and his colleague Lance-Bombardier W.H. Appleton of Ashington was killed when a truck plunged over a ravine.

Matty spent time in an Athens hospital before re-joining his regiment in Crete. He was involved in fighting the German invaders in the mountains and at the coast near Canea. He was one of 280 Yeomen from the Hussars who were issued with rifles and ordered to defend the coast of Crete. They endured three weeks of bitter fighting holding out against relentless air attacks by the Germans. Then on the 20th May looking towards Canea they saw hundreds of aircraft, fighters, and Junkers 52s towing gliders which dropped thousands of German paratroopers near the Hussars positions. On the 27th May an allied withdrawal was issued and by the 31st May orders to capitulate and make contact with the enemy. Matty was now one of over 12,000 prisoners of war taken after the Battle of Crete.

Matty and his mates of C Company who survived were shipped away on a seven day journey below decks to Salonika in Greece before being

Matty in the centre holding the shovel pictured with his marras underground at Ellington Colliery before he left to join the Hussars.

83

crammed into cattle trucks and interred in the infamous prisoner of war camp there. Many of the prisoners were starving by then and what was to come just as bad. Old filthy buildings infested with rats and bugs that caused many to sleep outside. Rations were a meagre pint of watery soup a day with a piece of bread or biscuit. Anyone attempting to escape received no mercy. After a few weeks in Salonika the troops were rounded up and herded through the streets before being ordered into railway wagons, thirty-six men to each truck unable to even lie down. The heat was intense and the men only allowed out for five minutes every twelve hours. No sanitary arrangements at all and some of the prisoners ill and suffering from diarrhoea meant appalling conditions.

Trooper Matty Willis in Hussars uniform.

Matty was interred in a German prison camp which was probably Stalag VIIIB where life though hard was much easier and he became friends with an Australian prisoner named Les Miller. In poor health by then Matty was taken seriously ill and spent some time in a German hospital before being repatriated via Sweden and then sent back home. His friend Les was also repatriated near the end of the war and came to stay with Matty's family in Lynemouth before heading home to Australia.

The people of Lynemouth gave Matty a great welcome home after his repatriation where he and his family were guests of honour at a social evening held in Lynemouth Hotel. A cheque for £5 was presented to Trooper Willis by Mrs Gordon, Honorary Secretary of the Women's section of the British Legion, who organised the event and supported by the Legion Men's section. This social event was reported in the Morpeth Herald on 26th November 1943.

The Allies War Grave Cemetery near Sucla Bay in Crete where many of Matty's comrades rest.

This was not the end of the war for Matty, as when he recovered he trained as a motorcycle courier and was sent to Guernsey. It was then when home on leave he met his wife to be Mary and they corresponded until he was demobbed after the end of the war and they married in 1947 when Matty returned to work at Ellington Colliery.

Over the years Matty and Mary have visited Crete many times to pay their respects to Matty's fallen comrades in the dark days of the Second World War.

Left: Back to work at Ellington Colliery Matty is yoking up his pony in the underground shaft stables.

Jim Pegg's Testimony

I joined the Royal Engineers and left Lynemouth to go to war in April 1940. I took part in the ill fated Norwegian campaign and during the retreat to the coast at Lillehammer our train was hit by a land mine. Our section were in the first wooden car behind the engine and it disintegrated as more cars piled on top. Fires spread out as dive bombers attacked the wreckage. With other severely injured men I was carried to a nearby house. We were captured by the Germans a few hours later, it was 1st May 1940.

Meting Olga

After recovering from my injuries I was sent to POW camps in Poland and then in 1942 taken to work on the farm of Bruno Wargentin in West Prussia. Polish labourers were being replaced by slave labourers from the Ukraine. One of these workers caught my eye, a young woman by the name of Olha Yutschenko forever to be known to me as Olga. There was a sadness about her that her big green eyes and regal bearing failed to hide. Fairly proficient in speaking German I soon picked up the rudiments of Ukrainian and Olga and I became good friends. Ten year old Ukrainian slave Michsuka or Mickey to us would shuttle back and forth with messages between Olga and me. She had been one of the victims of Stalin's famine in the Ukraine and had been left as a nine year old to care for her two young sisters while her mother left to search for food. They died in her arms before her mother returned.

Proposal Under Fire

Sunday, 3rd October 1943 with Mickey keeping watch for guards I met Olga for a few minutes behind a barn. Suddenly the quiet of the day was rent asunder by waves of hundreds of aircraft winging in low over the town of Marienberg just across the River Nogat near Schanua. They dropped their bombs on the new Focke-Wolfe aircraft factory. While they thundered overhead and the ground shook beneath us from the high explosives I proposed to Olga. She said yes and as the bombs rained down we said our vows to God and to each other. Some of the aircraft returned and dropped what I

Mickey, the slave boy, who ran with messages between Jim and Olga.

laughingly said was confetti to bless our marriage but later knew to be propaganda leaflets. It was then that we decided we would attempt to escape from the farm and find our way to safety.

Escape and Capture

Over the following months I saved cigarettes from my Red Cross parcels and Olga was able to collect a full set of Cossack clothes for me. We escaped and found an abandoned farmhouse with other slave workers who hid out there. Some of them at night looted abandoned German houses. Ten days later we were all captured when the farm was surrounded by black clad SS men. Those that were found to have looted possessions were lined up and shot. Olga and I were only saved from the firing squad as we had not taken part in any looting.

The Lieutenant who drove us to Dirschau Concentration Camp knew by my speech I was not from the Ukraine but introduced us to the camp commandant as Ivan and Olga Yurtschenko, husband and wife who had been interrogated by the SS and cleared. The Nazis thought slave workers inhuman but allowed husbands and wives to stay together so we were taken to a hut reserved for married couples. I had to concoct a story to cover for my limited knowledge of the Ukrainian language. I told the interrogators that I had been born in Finland of Ukrainian parents and was orphaned at an early age and brought up in a Finnish orphanage which accounted for my poor command of the Ukrainian language. The following day all able bodied men were set to work clearing snow from the streets of Dirschau and I met up and became friends with Andre a grizzled old Cossack from Rostov who warned me not to speak Ukrainian to other Ukraine prisoners and stick to speaking German. He had heard my 'fairy' story and suspected I was British but said my secret was safe with him.

Desperate Days

A few days later we were all herded into cattle cars and taken to Gdansk and stayed locked inside the cars overnight at the railyards. Next morning we were marched off in a raging blizzard in the direction of Gdynia. We were given no food but Olga had saved a chunk of bread that helped to sustain us during that dreadful march. Prisoners who dropped from fatigue were left to die in the 30 degree below zero cold and drifting snow. Those of us who survived staggered into a camp near Gdynia and were placed in a hut with barely room to sit.

Olga sat with her back against the hut wall when a prisoner pulled her away and sat there himself. I berated him in German and a guard came over and threw him outside. The guard then left but returned with a bowl of soup for us which we shared with Andre and a young French girl named Helene. Next day Olga and I were assigned to a hut reserved for families.

Each morning we were sent to a place where the German army was building a new line of defence and we worked 14 hours a day digging anti tank trenches. Our only meal was at the end of the day, a slice of bread and half a pint of watery soup.

Prisoners too ill to work received no food and were left to die. After a few days of hard labour I had missed seeing Andre. That evening I saved some soup and went to his quarters and found him close to death. I tried to spoon feed him but he whispered to me. 'You eat it you will need it to survive if you are to get Olga back to England.' He died in my arms and I covered him with his tattered old coat. I said the Lord's Prayer and quietly promised Andre I would indeed get Olga to England.

Narrow Escape

The Soviet airforce began pounding the new defence line with bombs and bullets and during these raids we threw ourselves on the ground and covered our heads with our shovels. After one heavy raid Olga and I struggled to our feet but Helene working beside us lay prostrate. I turned her over but she had gone, her body riddled with machine gun bullets. I covered her face with her scarf and said the Lord's Prayer as Olga stood silently weeping.

Jim during his first year as a prisoner. A photo taken by his Nazi captors when the Red Cross provided a new uniform.

In the fields through which we marched to work, farmers had stored piles of potatoes covered with straw and earth and we sometimes broke ranks to stick our hands through the layers and grab a potato which we devoured like apples. But one night at the camp gates we were searched and five men and five women were found to possess plundered potatoes. They were led away and in the morning they were hanged on makeshift gallows in front of assembled prisoners. A sign hung from a second row of makeshift gallows which read 'For future plunderers'.

A few days later twenty of us men were taken to a cliff and put to work digging a tunnel which was intended to be used as the German 2nd Army headquarters. I was amazed when a German sergeant came up to me and said. 'It is Jim isn't it.' I realised it was Franz whom I had met four years earlier in hospital in far off Norway. He asked me why I was here and I decided to trust him and tell the truth. Each day Franz would bring a little extra food in his haversack for Olga and me and made arrangements with his regiment cook to supply Olga with a large pot and ingredients to make soup for all the tunnel workers.

One morning all male prisoners were ordered to prove who they were as some of the Germans fearful of retribution by the advancing Red Army had changed into clothes of prisoners who had been killed. I had no way of proving my claim of being a Ukrainian and was deemed a deserter and lined up with other men facing another firing squad. Then Olga burst through the ranks threw her arms around me shouting 'They will have to shoot me too'. Hearing her speak Ukrainian the officer in command pointed at us and said 'Rauss' which means go. As we hurried away shots rang out behind us.

Escape and Danger

We were worked at night to try and escape the losses inflicted by the Red Army but came under heavy cannon fire one evening and we all ran in disarray. Fires lit up the sky. Gydinia and Gdansk were burning as we passed German soldiers hanging from bridges and trees. They had been executed by the SS for 'Refusing to fight for the Fatherland', many of them were just boys. We passed the camp gates and the gallows then midst all this death, disease, hunger and fear in this desolate land something amazing happened. I sensed a light around me and heard a small voice which said 'Do not be afraid for I am with you' and I knew then that God had spoken and was watching over me.

The following night at the cliff with the guns sounding ever nearer I took Olga by the arm and we scrambled over the sides of the anti tank ditches and ran east towards the guns. We hid in a forest surviving on ice and grass until we were spotted by a Red Army patrol and taken to an internment camp at Neudeck. Later two Englishmen were interred in the camp, Raymond Stamp from Whitley Bay and Harry Dimmock from the Midlands, so at last I could converse in English again.

Boris the camp Kommandant had an aversion to the west and had classed us as criminals and alerted the Soviet Secret Police. When Ivan who was a Christian replaced him he could not release us because of this situation. It was then that while accompanying Ivan on a visit to his headquarters that Olga faced a dangerous situation. The lieutenant who Ivan left in charge was drinking with the guards and said they could have their way with the women. Harry and Raymond had fought off the drunken guards until the women locked themselves into a windowless room. Ivan had his second in command stripped of his rank and locked up.

A Pass To Freedom

It was time to go and we escaped again with Harry and Raymond and reached Touron hoping to board a train to Warsaw. We needed passes from the local Soviet Kommandant and it was Harry and Raymond who obtained these from the Kommandant's secretary as fortunately her boss was away on other business.

We rode to Warsaw on top of a coal car arriving dirty and hungry and made our way through the ruins of a once beautiful city. Then suddenly out of the smoke came a wonderful sight, an American jeep flying the stars and stripes. We ran out into the road and hailed none other than Colonel William Mckee Dunne, American Military Attache. He gave us a lift to the Hotel Polonial where the British Embassy staff were being installed that very day.

We met the embassy staff, Freddy Wall and Freddy Russell, in the foyer and they asked us grubby looking tramps who we were. 'We are esaped prisoners of war and this is Olga Yurtschenko she escaped with me and I am taking her back to England.' The authorities in England were notified, then the Ambassodor said that Olga and I should get married as soon as possible. This would make her a British citizen in their eyes if not in the eyes of the Soviets.

Marriage and Home

It was not easy to find a Protestant minister in Catholic Poland but eventually we found a man standing by the ruins of a Methodist Chapel. He was Pastor Jesakow who brought his senior, Pastor Naider who asked us questions and told us to come back in three days while they cleared the debris from the ruined chapel. We were married on the 25th July 1945 with Raymond as best man and it was he who supplied a wedding ring he had made from a German penny.

Olga and Jim on their wedding day in Warsaw, 25th July 1945. Jim is wearing an American officer's uniform which helped them cross the Red Army checkpoint before boarding the plane for home.

After the ceremony a lovely surprise awaited us. Ambassador Sir Cavendish Bentinck had arranged a wedding feast in the Embassy and invited staff from the other allied embassies to join us.

The British government thought the only chance of smuggling Olga out would be by plane as there were too many Red Army checkpoints to negotiate by road to Berlin. After many requests the Russians gave permission for a plane to land in Warsaw but how to get us from the embassy to the airfield was another problem. It was the American ambassador who loaned us his car and chauffeur. I was dressed in an American officer's uniform and Olga given a new set of clothes. The chauffeur drove straight past the Red Army guards at the airfield and seeing my officers uniform saluted as we passed and I returned the gesture in true military fashion. The engines of the Lancaster bomber were roaring as we pulled alongside and we were quickly bundled inside the open door and airborne within seconds. After re-fuelling in Copenhagen we crossed the North Sea and the young pilot brought the plane down below the cloud cover and said to me. 'There she is Jim,' and when I looked out there she was indeed, the green fields and hedgerows of England.

Editor: Jim and Olga Pegg came home to Lynemouth after the war then emigrated to Canada in 1954. Olga died at Warkworth, Ontario in 1994 never losing her faith in the Lord. They had two daughters Anne and Jeannette. Two years later Jim married Dorothy Pratt, both were lay ministers with Warkworth Free Methodist Church. Jim dedicated his life to Christ at a mission service at Lynemouth in the 1930s and carried his faith for the rest of his life.

Another Lynemouth man who was a POW during the Second World War was Fred Harding, seen on the back right of this picture as member of the concert party at Stalag IXC. Fred loved a sing song and was known to take to the stage back home at Lynemouth Club. Machine gun crew member, Fred was captured fighting after the first Dunkirk invasion. Like his father Fred before him in the First World War he had campaigned with the Northumberland Fusiliers in the Second World War.

Jack Patrick's Wartime Memories

Our family lived in 71 Albion Terrace where my dad, George Robert, had his grocers shop. He had been a regular soldier before the war and served as a trooper with the 13th-18th Hussars in Egypt. When war was declared in 1939, he became a member of the Lynemouth Home Guard. I remember as a child, stacks of ammunition being stored behind our front door. They used the Welfare ground for training purposes and one Sunday there was a public demonstration involving a Bren Gun Carrier. A member of the Home Guard showed how to attach a 'sticky bomb' to a steel hopper in a rough area of the Welfare ground.

George Robert Patrick, second from right in the back row, of his Home Guard unit at the start of the Second World War, before being called up for service in 1942.

Dad was called up around 1942 joining the RASC and sent overseas to fight. He was captured and became a prisoner for the rest of the war in one of the infamous German prison camps. My mam was left to care for my brother Robert and me as well as running the shop. At first we had no air raid shelter and when the air raid buzzer sounded we hid under the stairs. One night when we hid there in the dark, came a terrific bang and the whole house shook.

Robert grabbed hold of Mam and shouted, 'What's that Mam?'

'Its Hitler knocking at our door', came the reply.

'Don't let him in then, mam, don't let him in.'

During another raid we watched incendiary bombs flaring over Lynemouth Colliery and I remember the damaged and demolished buildings in Albion Terrace and Dalton Avenue. The newly built Albion Post Office was completely flattened. There was lots of wood amongst the damaged houses and many of the older lads made stilts from the salvaged beams.

In 1944 Mam was in Morpeth and as darkness fell she stepped off the footpath to look up at the clock tower. A police car came around the corner and struck her, breaking her leg. She was a victim of the blackout and taken to Ashington Hospital. Robert and I were sent to stay with our grandparents in Castle Terrace, Ashington. When we visited Mam in hospital we were not allowed on the ward – we had to look through a door and wave to her.

At home Robert and me had a collection of pieces of shrapnel from the shells fired at the German aircraft. We found these in the street and one big piece was found in our back yard. One occasion I can still remember clearly is when I was an infant in Miss Fosters' class at Lynemouth School in 1944. When the air raid siren was sounded we children were ushered to the air raid shelters on the school green. We had to hold hands and stay together. Ann the girl I held hands with later became my wife and we are still together after all these years – 'Good old Hitler.'

My dad never talked about the war after the terrible things he had seen cleaning up in Hitler's death camps and never claimed his medals. I put that right later and now have his medals which he richly deserved and proudly wear them on ANZAC Day.

Editor: Jack and his wife Ann emigrated to New Zealand in the 1960s.

Back Home

Lynemouth's highly regarded Ashington Coal Company doctor, Tom Skene, is on the left supervising the after war celebrations in 1945 down the back street of the odd numbered Dalton Avenue and lower Albion Terrace.

The children of the odd numbered Dalton Avenue and lower Albion Terrace gathered together in front of the back yard walls of the Dalton colliery house.

Lynemouth was awash with street parties after the war with the residents of every row or block taking the chance to celebrate the end of the conflict. The villagers shown here are from Park Road and the top rows of Henley and Guilford and include members of the Brotherton and Snowdon families.

Supervised by parents, these youngsters from the area around Eden Terrace are all seated and ready for tea at the VE Day celebrations in 1945. Robert Patrick is sitting front left and opposite with the hat is Billy Waddell.

It took some time before local brass bands regrouped with some members drifting back after serving their country during the war and everyday life got back to normal. By September 1952 Ellington Colliery Silver Prize Band was in fine form winning first prize in the fourth section of the Daily Herald National Tribute held at Belle Vue, Manchester.

Below: The band continued winning trophies in the 1950s with success at the Annual Miners' Picnic held at Bedlington. Bandsmen and supporters stand proudly in front of the banner of the Ellington Branch of the NUM.

Ellington electrician, Alan Little, and Ellington Deputy, Bill Thompson, at Bedlington Picnic in the 1950s with their instruments at the ready to blow away the opposition.

Ellington Colliery

Before the laying out of the railway system from Linton to the proposed new site of Ellington Colliery in 1907 it was necessary to construct two bridges. One to cross over the Ashington road at Ellington Bank and the other a short distance away to cross over the River Lyne as it flowed into Ellington Dene.

Construction well underway to build a bridge over the River Lyne. These Ashington Coal Company workmen take time out to pose for the camera, circa 1907. Some of these men went on to join the Ellington Colliery shaft sinking team. The man on the left with trilby hat and a tie is obviously the 'Gaffer' and the boy sitting next to him would probably be messenger and tea boy for the team.

The River Lyne as it flows through the two tunnel bridge and on into Ellington Dene. Built with Ashington Coal Company bricks, the bridge has forever been known to locals as 'The Two Tunnels'. The workmen on the top are finishing off the coping slabs. The railway route across the bridge can be seen at the

very top of picture. This site was one of many in the area chosen and used to feature in the Billy Elliot film. A favourite place for spotting wildlife including otter, mink, kingfisher, grey wagtail and, in the Dene, red squirrel and great spotted woodpecker.

Ellington Colliery in 1915 and coal production well underway but still much work to be done on the surface buildings.

Circa 1928 and in the forefront the Colliery Institute erected in 1924 and still in business today. In the background the shaft towers and pulley wheels of the Betty and Number Two Pit look out over the winding houses. At the Institute in March 1926 a masked ball was held with 160 people involved. The winner of first prize for dress was none other than the pit manager, Mr A.E. Holliday!

The newly built Ellington Colliery Bath House and canteen in 1924. These were the first pit baths to be opened in the County. Workers at all the Ashington Coal Company pits paid a penny per week from their wages to see this happen.

The new Ellington Colliery Banner was designed in 1950 by former Ellington miner and founder of the Pitmen Painters group, Oliver Kilbourn. One of its first outings was at the Lynemouth Children's Gala Day escorted by pit and union officials seen here at Lynemouth School. Ernie Shears is holding the rope and behind him are Jim Laidler, Wilson Meredith and Andy McGlaughlan. Bill Sweet is kneeling front and pit manager Bill Wilkinson behind.

Left: Ellington Colliery Band had many successes in competition and boasted three regular young girls in their ranks. Sitting beside the Ellington Banner at Northumberland Miners' Gala in the 1950s are Lynemouth lasses fom the left: Winnie Cowton, Margaret Teasdale and Olive Graham.

Prizes in Section A at the 1953 Miners' Gala at Bedlington are shown off by Ellington band members and followers

The old Lynemouth Welfare Pavilion provided the backdrop for these Ellington Colliery craftsmen who held a Fitters versus Electricians cricket match in the 1950s. Back row: Addy Brown, R. Mitchell, Billy Kidd, Ray Barron, ?, ?. Middle row: ?, ?, Gordon Proctor, George Shepherd, Tommy Thompson, M. McSparron, Danny Peary, Bob Thompson, Ken Hanson. Sitting: ?, Alan Little, Raymond Railston, ?, Jimmy Jacques, Bill Scott, Jimmy Richardson.

Ellington Colliery was noted for turning out highly trained and competitive First Aid teams who regularly came home with silverware when competing in the Northern Area Coal Board competitions. Their trainer was the Coal Board's respected Ashington Training Centre instructor, Wilfy Dick. The successful Ellington team are standing at the back with mentor, Wilfy fourth from left.

The colliery as it was during a surface revamp and modernisation in 1956 but with the old boilerhouse chimney still intact at this stage, sitting close by the new winding house. The top of the shaft tower can be seen at the rear above the heapstead.

25th January 2005 and a last shift march out was held when Ellington Colliery closed. Ellington men led by union leaders march from the pithead to the Institute where the Ellington band played the miners requiem 'Gresford'.

Start of the demolition of the colliery and the end for the boilerhouse chimney

Ellington Colliery Memorial

Ellington Colliery Memorial was unveiled on the 7th November 2009 by then President of the NUM, Ian Lavery, and former pit manager, Jack Tubby, to commemorate the workforce from 1909-2005. It is the product of a dedicated committee that worked for almost two years to raise funds and enable the sculpture to be completed by local sculptor, Tom Maley. Considered by many to be the finest local mining memorial they have seen, it stands as a testament to the last deep mine to be worked in the North East coalfield.

It has open access to the public and is used as a focal point in mining history and heritage for schools, organisations and indeed anyone who wishes to visit. Heritage talks and tours can be arranged by contacting the memorial committee. The memorial appears on the Ellington Parish website. Since its erection in 2009, the sculpture is lit up in the hours of darkness and has 24 hour surveillance. At the present time the memorial committee are liaising with Harworth estates and prospective purchasers of the former UK Coal Ellington Colliery land to secure the future of the site. Information panels were put in place with funding from UK Coal and, when the land is eventually secured, memorial members will be raising funds towards landscaping the area and providing easy access for visitors to the site.

Pictured outside their headquarters members of the memorial group pose with the sculptor and mini memorial prior to the unveiling day. Back row: Eileen Brown, Jim Sawyer, Stan Elliot, Jack Boaden, Barry Mead. Front row: Milburn Douglas, Tom Maley, Neil Taylor, Jack Tubby, Peter Wood.

Sculptor Tom Maley on the left and his assistant preparing the base and siting the memorial prior to the opening ceremony on 7th November 2009.

Local MP, Alan Beith, stands with the Ellington Colliery Band as they play an introduction to the memorial opening.

A varied programme of events followed the memorial opening ceremony and one of the attractions were children from Michelles School of Dance who entertained a packed audience in the Ellington Miners' Social Centre.

A sculpture with a meaning as the miner is looking east into the rising sun facing a new future, yet holding on to the past as he touches the fallen shaft tower pulley wheel.

Ellington Colliery and Village

Jessie Rich who now lives in Sussex has fond memories of Ellington and Cresswell and looks back at her heritage: 'My Grandfather Edward Matthews was born at Lesbury in 1868 and moved to Ellington Colliery in 1910 after previously working for Armstrong's at Newcastle and on the Forth Bridge. He became head blacksmith at Ellington Colliery and retired at the age of 75 sometime during the Second World War. I believe a man named Danny Peary succeeded him as head blacksmith.

'The Third Row at Ellington Colliery was then known as Inglewood Terrace and the family lived at number six. After a few years the name of the street was changed to just plain Third Row and the houses were re-numbered from the opposite end which now meant they were living at no 13 Third Row. In number 12 were the Elliot family and the Proctors in number 14. Later the Bob Bell family lived in number 12.

'My mother, who sadly died in 2005 aged 96, often talked about life at Ellington and Cresswell and the good times they had. I myself have such happy memories of those places and feel privileged to have lived there.'

Jessie's grandfather is among these retired Ashington Group Mechanics being given a souvenir of the Inaugaral Retirements Grants Pension Concert on 11th November 1949. These momentos were given by the Ashington and Woodhorn Colliery Mechanics Benevolent Fund Committee. Members pictured, left to right: W. Wharrier (Fund Chairman), J. McFarlane (Woodhorn Colliery mechanic), T. Lowrie (retired Ashington member), R. Wallace (Ashington Colliery Mechanics and Benevolent Fund Sec), K. Johnson (retired Woodhorn Colliery member), G. Stobbart (retired Linton Colliery member), E. Matthews (retired Ellington Colliery member).

Young Sadie Scott moved with her mining family from Widdrington to Ellington Colliery. She is pictured here during the First World War giving her pet dog a ride in an old pram.

Right: Ellington ran a football team in the early years of the 20th century and played in the field across from the pit and opposite First Row. This field also doubled as a summer sports venue where foot racing was held and organised by Ellington men.

The Statham family had just moved into the Colliery rows in the 1920s when Fred and little sister Josie played out in the security of the back yard with this mobile elephant. At the rear of the yard, walls built with Coal Company bricks in 1909 are in pristine condition.

Ellington & District Sports,
HELD SEPT. 13th, 1913.

Secretary : J. WADDELL, 1st Row, Ellington.
Handicapper & Referee : J. HEDLEY. Pistol Firer : B. WALKER.

100 Yards Youth's Handicap

First £1, Second 10/-, Third 5/-, Fourth 2/6.

HEAT 1 at 2 o'clock p.m.	Yrs.	Yds.	HEAT 5	Yrs.	Yds.
1 J Pollard, Ellington	14	17	1 A Dodds, Morpeth	13	15
2 R Burn, Hirst	8	20	2 M Downs, Ashington	13	13
3 R Furness, Hirst	15	10½	3 L Key, Hirst	15	11½
4 E Mordue, Hirst	11	22	4 G Thompson, Ashington	7	31
5 A Donaldson, Hirst	13	18	5 W Lothian, Morpeth	11	19
HEAT 2.			HEAT 6.		
1 J Baxter, Linton	10	27	1 G Brown, Sunderland	*	6½
2 Isaac Charlton, Hirst	12	20½	2 J Hall, Ellington	17	13
3 G Collins, Newbiggin	14	14	3 C Cook, Morpeth	16	10
4 H Fenwick, Hirst	15	13	4 E Adey, Hirst	12	18½
5 R Grieves, New Moor	*	15	5 A Tipton, Hirst	14	15½
HEAT 3.			HEAT 7.		
1 G Harvey, South Linton	12	18½	1 G Jones, Ferneybeds	18	8
2 T Horn, Linton	12	22	2 Jas Murray, Morpeth	13	16½
3 T Soulsby, Morpeth	14	13	3 J Edwards, Broomhill	14	14
4 R Scott, Ellington	18	10	4 R Bowart, (L Brow Ash)	13	13
5 J Williams, Ellington	13	18	5 E Egglestone, Cleadon	13	*
HEAT 4			HEAT 8.		
1 R Smith, Hirst	12	18	1 R Patterson, Ferneybeds	14	12
2 J Robson, Ellington	18	10½	2 R McGee, Hirst	13	15
3 F Adey, Hirst	6½	30	3 A Henstock, Newbiggin	12	18
4 T Beattie, Amble	*	6	4 T Young, East Chop'ton	12	18
5 J Jackson, Hirst	8	26			

Winners of Heats fall as follows :
1st Tie—1 2 3 4 ; 2nd Tie—5 6 7 8
1st and 2nd in each Tie to run in Final.

1st Heat of 120-yds. to follow after the Ties of Youths'.

120 Yards Novice Handicap

(OPEN.) First £5, Second £2, Third 15/-, Fourth 5/-.

HEAT 1.	Yds.	HEAT 5.	Yds.
1 R Gray, Ellington	15	1 C H Close, Newbiggin	14½
2 J Coe, Ashington	14½	2 T Jackson, Amble	10
3 F Hunter, Hirst	14	3 R Taylor, Ellington	17
4 C Cook, Morpeth	15	4 T Pringle, Ulgham	15½
HEAT 2,		HEAT 6.	
1 G Robinson, Ellington	12	1 J Robson, Ellington	17
2 J W Bell, Ulgham Manor	15½	2 B Burton, Hirst	15½
3 J Morris, Hirst	13½	3 G Brown (late Bell), Sunderland	12
4 J Davidson, Broomhill	15	4 H Gouton, Hirst	16
HEAT 3.		HEAT 7.	
1 G Jones, Ferneybeds	13½	1 R Scott, Ellington	17
2 J Taylor, Ashington	14½	2 T Nelson, Ashington	10
3 G Mavin, Ellington	17	3 W Tait, Ashington	14
4 T Smailes, Hauxley	12½	4 S Kirkup, Ashington	17
HEAT 4.		HEAT 8.	
1 G Robinson, Stobswood	12	1 W Simpson, Linton	12
2 W Coulson, Linton	17	2 M Brady, Ashington	14
3 G Curry, Ulgham Village	15½	3 T Chapman, South Shields	10½
4 R Smith, Hirst	14½	4 T Athey, New Moor	14

Winners of heats fall as follows :
1st Tie—1 2 , 3 4 ; 2nd Tie—5 6 7 8
1st and 2nd in Ties to run in Final.

Ellington folk had a reputation for staging concerts and celebrating special events. This 1920s photo shows one of those events when these young boys posed for the camera in the village vicarage garden. Back row: Bill Charlton, unknown, John Crawford, George Jacques. Front row: Jimmy Bell, Frank Harrington, John Holland.

An early 1920s snap of Ellington youngsters posing after a concert. Annie Matthews is back left in dark clothing and then Violet Statham who went on to organise all the local children's plays, pantomimes and concerts.

A memorable year for any young girl when crowned a Gala Queen. This photo taken in the late 1940s sees the Ellington girl chosen sitting amongst her admiring attendants in the Ellington vicarage garden.

Ellington Colliery Institute Saturday night dance was a mecca for the young folk of the area. Each year a Miss Ellington competition was held and many local girls from the mining families would take part. Here is one attractive young lady that took the eye of the judges during that 1950s era. Elaine Davidson, a miner's daughter from Lynemouth, was declared a unanimous winner and is seen here wearing the Miss Ellington sash.

PROGRAMME.

"Bold Robin and The Babes"

AN OPERETTA

IN FOUR SCENES.   BY COHYER ROWE.

Scene 1 .... A Village Green
Scene 2 ....A Forest (Evening)
Scene 3 .... A Dame's School
Scene 4 .... A Forest Scene

Between Scenes 1 and 2

Violin Solo .... Master F. Statham

Between Scenes 2 & 3 and 3 & 4

Solos   ....   Miss Jessie Mitchell

     At the Piano ... ... MRS. G. HALL

     Violin ... ... MR. PURVIS, L.C.M.

DRAMATIS PERSONÆ.

Jack } The Babes of ... { Fred Statham
Jill } the Wood ... { Edith Davison
Village Crier ... ... John Keen
Job Trot ... ...   Sadie Storey
Eliza Trot ... ...   Margaret Hetherington
Village Schoolmistress ... ... Connie Brown
Fairy Queen ... ... Mary Little
Puck, Attendant on Queen ... Margaret Park
Robin Hood ... ...   Billy Ellerington

FAIRIES.
M. Hetherington, S. Strachan, E. Waddell, M. Herron, F. Scott, M. Hall, G. Tait, E. Robson, M. Keen, N. Keen, M. Statham, N. Bell, E. Strachan.

MERRY MEN OF SHERWOOD.
J. Keen, J. Kerr, R. Wilson, T. Holland, J. Brown, T. Bell, R. Redhead, Fred Statham.

GOD SAVE THE KING.

The cast for a programme of entertainment given by the children of Cresswell Parish Sunday School. It was held at Ellington Colliery Institute for three nights with a matinee for children.

Ellington children who attended a Christmas tea and concert, circa 1954. The boy bottom left of picture is TV darts presenter Sid Waddell. Sadly Sid died in 2012 after a battle with cancer.

A pantomime at Ellington Institute, circa 1948, with some names from Mrs Statham's concert remembered: Dot Wilshire, Jean Strachan, Isobel Nicholson, Brenda Lucas, Ralph Tait, Dave Harvey, Alan Robson, Rowell, Ridley.

Above: Ellington Ladies Club has provided a Christmas concert and dinner for all Ellington residents of pension age for many years. Here are some of the early club members performing on stage. Left to right: Jo Tipple, Gladys Blake, Pat Taylor, Audrey Patrick, Betty Douglas, ?, Sheila English, Phoebe Jacques, Mary Fairbairn, Kathleen Robson.

Left: Schoolteacher Gordon Thompson of Ellington suffered a spinal injury when out climbing in the Northumbrian hills which changed his life completely. Ellington Ladies Club and family seen here with Gordon rallied round to help by raising the sum of £400 in a funding appeal set up by Gordon's friends. Gordon, no mean artist, held an exhibition of his paintings at Morpeth Town Hall.

Man of the People

Ellington man, ex-Police Inspector Alan Evans, had many strings to his bow. A military man before joining the Police Force, Alan then a sergeant was chosen to receive the Nation's Community Policeman of the Year award in September 1993 for his community work in North Shields' Meadowell Estate after the riots there in 1991. Then more accolades followed as Prime Minister John Major recommended further honours to the Queen, and Alan received an MBE in the 1994 New Year's Honours List.

After retirement, keen hockey player Alan and leading light of Morpeth Hockey club, immersed himself in family life and the Ellington Community. Well known for producing hilarious sketches and videos for Ellington Ladies Group, the ladies blessed him with a further title and one of which he was extremely proud. The only male ever to become 'Honarary member of Ellington Ladies Group.' Alan's input to the community is greatly missed.

Alan Evans receives his country's Community Policeman of the Year award from Prime Minister John Major.

Alan in his community role on the Meadowell Estate, forging a bond with the local youngsters and explaining what could be done to improve relations between the residents and the police.

Ellington Ladies committee pictured at their annual dinner. They included Alan as an honorary member of their group.

105

Ellington Village

Ellington is an old Saxon village. The name means 'Ella's River Town' as Ella was a Saxon leader; Lin a Celtic word for river and a tun is a Saxon dwelling place. It was always known as an old farming community until the advent of coal and the sinking of Linton Colliery from 1894 and Ellington in 1909. Ashington Coal Company owned and farmed the land. With a large dairy herd grazing pasture around the area, the Company at one period during the early 20th century became the fifth largest milk producer in the country.

The local distribution farm for this area was East Moor Dairy, situated just outside Ellington Village. This gave employment to local women at the dairy and local lads who delivered bottled milk by horse and cart to households in the expanding mining villages.

For the delivery lads it meant an early start around 5 am as milk was expected by customers on the doorstep before breakfast. I remember as a young lad two of my older friends, Geordie Cleverley and Harry Shears, who worked milk rounds and I helped them on many occasions. Bike was the means of transport to the dairy from Lynemouth or sometimes a foray through Ellington Dene, then over fields on a more direct route in the summer.

It was working with horses that really attracted me to these early morning eye openers. I loved the smell and warmth of the stables when harnessing the horses and leading them out to yolk up to the milk cart. Often in the winter they would shake their harness, toss their heads and snort great clouds of steam into the frosty air.

The Plough in Ellington Village, built in 1802 and later extended. The first licencee of the Plough was Mr W. Hallowell and there are still Hallowells in the village at time of writing. Times have changed since the spit and sawdust days when the 'Plough', which did cater for travellers in the early years, was mainly open to cater for local bar trade. Today, the new tenant welcomes local trade but also specialises in meals and bed and breakfast accommodation.

An Ellington Colliery workers' day trip in the 1920s started from the Plough Inn. Pictured here the men are posing inside and outside a Coal Company charabanc prior to lift off to a venue unknown. What is known is that the man with the Fez is Ellington man, Tom Johnson.

A 1926/7 Ellington School class photo shows Mrs Fletcher on the left who ruled her pupils with an iron rod and sometimes with a cane. Alice Johnson is third left back row and Samuel Johnson, third left in the front row.

The school football team named themselves 'The Tigers' in 1932 and some of the boys are seen wearing black and yellow striped shirts. Samuel Johnson, shown centre of the back row, in his later years started a football club at Coulsdon in Surrey which became very successful.

Little has changed on the main frontage save for the closing down of the petrol pumps outside the Bank Top Stores. The shop was built as a Co-op in 1909 before falling into private hands. The pumps soon disappeared after Tom Mertens opened his garage nearby.

Tom Mertens built the Central Garage at Ellington in 1953. When Tom retired it was sold in the 1970s to George Hubb and then later sold on and demolished to make way for the new houses which now comprise Wytch Elm Close.

A 1950s postcard of Warkworth Lane Caravan Park as it was prior to development. Now a thriving business, open for residents for most of the year with its own clubhouse and games facilities.

Village Life

After years of negotiations over ownership, repairs and renovation, Ellington Village's old school house and county library was finally handed over to a local residents trust. It is now run solely by volunteers as a community village hall, café and library. These are some of the dedicated committee, councillors and helpers involved, pictured at the opening day on 23rd October 2010.

No dignitaries here to open the revamped Ellington Wildlife Pond on Easter Saturday 23rd April 2011. Seven local children were the ones chosen by the committee to perform the cutting of the ribbon. It was thought that this would encourage young people to use and learn about the benefits of the new wildlife facility.

Pond Dipping, Bird Ringing, as well as a host of wildlife exhibitions and stalls plus a free Hog Roast brought out the locals on a fine and dry day to the pond opening.

Memories of former school galas came flooding back when Ellington celebrated the Queen's Diamond Jubilee in June 2012 with a festive day at the village hall and grounds. Local man John Patterson was MC for the occasion introducing a varied programme of events ranging from fancy dress to pie eating. Seen here, John is taking time out to speak to residents and take in a little refreshment.

A line up of
Ellington
children
waiting
patiently for
the judging
of the
Jubilee fancy
dress
competition.

Lots of
young folk
entered for
the pie
eating
competition.
Sounds
easy but not
so and a bit
messy, but
loads of fun
when
hands are
not allowed
to be used.

A huge
interest in the
tug o' war
saw teams
comprising of
girls, boys,
men and
women
competing
with ages
ranging from
10 years to
over 50.

Ellington Juniors

Ellington Juniors Football Club was formed in 1988 and incorporates teams ranging from under 7s to under 21s. This means over 150 young people are representing Ellington in various football leagues and travelling to play as far away as Tyneside. Now having been gifted land by Alcan behind the allotment gardens, the committee have set out an exciting and ambitious plan to develop the land with a view to providing three football pitches and a club house with changing facilities. This would cement the future of Ellington Juniors for generations to come.

Above: Ellington Juniors under 11s side pictured at a tournament with coaches, John Farrell and Laura Blake.

Left: Ellington Juniors under 12s with coaches Ray and Trevor Dunn pictured after success at a Skegness Soccer Festival. Their medals were presented by former Newcastle favourite Kevin Keegan on left front of photo.

Right: Success for Ellington Juniors under 12s in the 2013-14 season, pictured here with their trophies when they won the League Challenge Cup, beating Monkseaton Blacks in the final at Wallsend.

CRESSWELL (local SPRING)
Traced back to Norman times
LOCAL Anglo Saxon allowed to
retain their lands.
A SAXON CROSS FOUND CLOSE
TO St BARTHOLOMEW'S CHURCH.
The Well on a boundary wall
on the village green. Within
the Ancient PELE TOWER.
PELE TOWER Now 14th century
ruins
17th century manor demolished in P112
1845.

...well or spring that supplied the villagers' water ...ides of the well hence the birth of the name ...me of Cresswell can be traced back as far as the ...d that they were Anglo Saxon and allowed to ...oss was found close to St Bartholomew's ...hat period in the village's history.

Pele Tower Cresswell 2

The well as it is and has been for centuries set in a boundary wall on the village green with the ancient Pele Tower of the Cresswell family in the background. It was not until the 1930s that Cresswell received a mains water supply.

The Pele Tower
(Scheduled Ancient Monument)
CRESSWELL HALL 1821-24
Stone from Cresswell from Snab
Point Quarry NZ 30080 92750
Via miniature railway
ESTATE sold off to Northumberland
County Council
Snab Point NZ 30379 92629
CRESSWELL STRONG FISHING TRAD
LIFEBOAT FROM 1875 - 1944
Named ELLEN and ELIZA.

The Cresswell Pele Tower as it stands today is mainly 14th century and was built on the site of an earlier fortification. The 17th century manor house and chapel that was built adjoining the Pele Tower was demolished in 1845. The Pele Tower is a Scheduled Ancient Monument and Grade Two listed building. Park Resorts own the Tower but the Parish Council are negotiating to have the ownership transferred to them and seeking funding to have a complete restoration with the blessing of English Heritage and the Heritage Lottery Fund. Much clearance work has already been done inside the tower by residents under the leadership of archaeologist and local historian, Barry Mead.

HEINKEL BOMBER SHOT DOWN 1941
DRURIDGE BAY.
CARGO SHIP 'EMPIRE BREEZE'
Ran aground at Hauxley
towed back by a tug which was hit
my a magnetic mine Sunk
in Bottom of Druridge Bay.
ROCK CUT HOLDING TANK
South side of THE OLD CRESSWELL
SEWER PIPE Kept Fish

...ver.

Left: The inside of the Pele Tower after being cleared of rubbish and weeds by Barry and his willing helpers from the village in August 2014. Some of the tower flagstones were missing and nothing of great archaeological value unearthed but the project is moving steadily forward.

In the 1930s Italian immigrant, Jimmy Padreddi, bought the end house of the newly built row seen here on the right with his motor car standing outside. The white building opposite is a wooden structure which he used as a café and dance hall until the new premises was fitted out ready for business as an ice cream parlour. The first real shop in Cresswell, later

tenanted by the Proctor family, it is still trading as Cresswell Ices with Brenda at the helm.

By the side of the Druridge coast road, between the Crow's Nest and the old Ellington Colliery Drift House, lies a once designated area for allotments allocated to Cresswell fishermen. From the 1930s the land was overgrown so plots of land were taken over by private landowners who built holiday bungalows for summer use. Now the bungalows have gone and previous owners difficult to trace. This area is at the present time a mecca for travelling families to occupy. The postcard shows the bungalows as they were in the 1930s.

The new Cresswell Hall built from 1821-24, designed in Grecian style by respected architect, John Shaw of London, and built by Mr Green of Newcastle. It was a huge legacy left to Addison John Cresswell's wife Elizabeth Mary Reed by her cousin John Baker that enabled the new hall and estate to evolve. This was the reason for the name change from Cresswell to Baker-Cresswell in 1840.

Cresswell Hall.

The main house boasted 24 rooms with a sophisticated underfloor heating system that kept the rooms at a pleasant 60 degrees Fahrenheit.

The stone for the inside of the hall was quarried at Cresswell and brought by a miniature railway that was laid from Snab Point Quarry to the building site of the new hall a mile away. The stone was not of sufficient quality to grace the outside of the hall. This material was shipped from Ashington and Cleasewell Hill Quarry. Some of the stones weighed as much as eight tons and some of these can still be seen today in the remains of the old colonnade that once connected the hall to a conservatory.

A separate building for servants and a state of the art stable block were situated at the north side of the hall. Parts of the stableyard clock tower and courtyard still remain but the magnificent hall was demolished in stages after the death of Addison Francis Cresswell in 1921 and the whole estate was sold off to Northumberland County Council in 1924.

There are many theories as to why the Cresswell siblings moved to pastures new after the death of their father, Addison Francis, but what is certain is that the hall and 111 acres of land was sold to Northumberland County Council. Proven to be structurally unsound, it was sold on to Ashngton Coal Company who owned the mineral rights in the late 1920s.

A 1907 picture of the luxurious fittings of the entrance hall and beyond the double stairway with Grecian figures and urns placed in prominent places. No expense was spared by the then wealthy Baker-Cresswell landlords.

The billiard room of Mr Baker Cresswell in which visiting male guests were entertained, tastefully decorated with murals, frescos and the finest fittings.

Cresswells, Baker-Cresswells and Widdringtons

The history of the Cresswell family and, from 1840, the Baker-Cresswell family has been well documented over the years. Yet as time moves on still more material comes to light, discovered by research and family involvement that gives a much more personal insight into the lives of the Cresswell dynasty.

The story of the last owner of Cresswell Hall, Addison Francis Baker-Cresswell is interesting to say the least. Addy, whose father died young, was sent to Eton to study and after the death of his grandfather inherited the Cresswell estates. He rented Cresswell Hall to his mother Lady Ravensworth as he spent much of his time at a London address and only came back to the area in the hunting season. He was master of the Percy foxhounds and kept 40 fine horses at the Cresswell stables.

In 1899 he married Ida Widdrington at Shillbottle Church, the daughter of Fitzherbert Widdrington of Newton Hall. They lived for a time at Harehope Hall, a Tudor style shooting lodge his grandfather had built, and then rented Inverary Castle from a friend for a short period. The marriage was not a happy one and eventually, after returning to Harehope, Ida moved on to live with her parents at Newton Hall before moving to Hauxley Hall which was owned by her father.

In 1903 Addy's mother caused a stir when she married her groom James Wadsworth in London before returning to Cresswell Hall. Addy died in 1921 and the whole of the Cresswell estate was sold off in 1924.

A sad ending which saw the eventual demolition of Cresswell Hall and the family involvement at Cresswell dating back at least 800 years.

Above: Harehope Hall near Edlingham, a fine Tudor hunting lodge built by the Cresswells then later owned by the Wrangham family and put up for sale in 2013.

Left: Joe Baker-Cresswell DSO, son of Addison Francis and Ida Widdrington. Joe helped to change the fortunes of war when, as Commander of 3rd Escort Group, his crew rescued an Enigma machine from a crippled German U-Boat in 1941. This helped to decode secret German messages. There was also a haul of documents and charts leading to U-Boat bases.

From 1914 many British regiments honed their skills for war when camped around the Cresswell area and some of the officers were housed in the Hall. Garden parties were still held in the grounds as shown here with this group of Ellington residents posing with a military guest.

Worth a Fortune

An eight by six foot oil painting that once graced the wall of the entrance vestibule in Cresswell Hall was the subject of a £4,000 bid by an art connoisseur in 1933. The painting, set in a carved wood frame, depicted John Addison Baker-Cresswell and his three sons, Oswin Addison, William Gilfred and Henry standing by the banks of a river. Dating from around 1840, it was thought to have been the commissioned work of a famous artist.

It was purchased for the sum of 10 shillings at a sale after the break up of the Cresswell estate in 1924 by the man who bought much of the Cresswell land, Alderman W.S. Sanderson of Morpeth. It was displayed in the Queen's Head, Morpeth and much admired by the public and art connoisseurs. It was one of those art lovers who made the bid of £4,000 which was rejected by Mr Sanderson.

The clock tower in the stable block and servants' quarters slowly decaying in the depths of Cresswell Wood.

A section of the once magnificent colonnade, that ran from the main hall to the conservatory, still remains intact.

Last of the Lifeboatmen

Cresswell with its situation at the south end of Druridge Bay maintains a strong fishing tradition. Today, there are still relatives of the original fishing families traced from the middle ages living in Southside, or Fishers Row as the cottages were once known.

Cresswell maintained a lifeboat service from 1875 until 1944. Three lifeboats were in service during that period. First the 'Old Potter' that was launched eight times from 1875 until 1889, with 33 lives saved. Then the 'Ellen and Eliza' from 1889 until 1909, launched 20 times with 41 lives saved. The last lifeboat to serve was the 'Martha' from 1909 until the station's closure in 1944. She was named after her benefactor Martha A. Vaughan of London.

A large turnout of people and the media came to see the first launch of the 'Martha' which came into service on 23rd September 1909.

Ellington Colliery electrician, Addison Brown, was a crew member of the 'Martha' when the station closed down in 1944. In 1992, aged 75 then living at Newbiggin, he became the last surviving member of the Cresswell lifeboatmen and gave an interview to the local press:

'The station at Cresswell was set up after a tragedy when my grandmother Kitty, who had never been out in a boat before, launched a boat in extreme weather in an attempt to reach her husband whose boat was in trouble when nearing the bay. Sadly, he died in the incident.

'Everyone involved with the lifeboat were volunteers and it was unique that during war years from the 1930s to the station closure in 1944, when my father Addison was coxain, all the crew were Browns which was a worry to the remaining family members on shore. The family even made the headlines in a magazine story in Buenos Aires in 1938 and I am still puzzled how the information found its way there.

'I was involved in two rescues – the first in 1941 involved a Heinkel bomber which was shot down over Druridge Bay. The second was the cargo ship 'Empire Breeze' which ran aground at Hauxley. As it was being towed back to the Tyne by a tug a magnetic mine

Coxain Addison Brown.

exploded sinking the tug, which I think is still at the bottom of Druridge Bay. Six people were taken to Ashington Hospital with serious scalds but the boat could not be towed away until the channel was swept for mines. Our lifeboat took 200 two gallon tanks out to the cargo ship to keep the pumps going until it could be towed to the Tyne. It was hard work in a ten-oared lifeboat, the oars were 14 foot long and stotted off your lifejacket.

'It took about 15 minutes to launch the lifeboat and all the villagers helped in this. Ironically none of the crew could swim and we relied entirely on our lifejackets.

'The last lifeboat at Cresswell – 'Martha' – was taken out of service in 1944 and sold privately. The last I heard of her was in 1980 when she had been converted into a houseboat down in Kent and aptly re-named 'The Cresswell'.'

Above: Cresswell vicar, the Reverend Thomas Horsfall, Honourary Secretary of the lifeboat, stands with Baroness Ravensworth of Cresswell Hall and a young girl all dressed for the historic occasion.

Left: At the water's edge after the launch, the crew prepare to give 'Martha' her first trial run in the bay.

Rock Cut Holding Tanks

Lying on the south side of the old Cresswell sewer pipe are four holding tanks, cut square into the rocks and visible at Low Tide. Of varying sizes, the largest measures

180 x 340 centimetres and has a depth of at least 40 cms, with slots in the top suggesting they could have been covered at sometime. Local knowledge confirms that they were covered, for this is where the Cresswell fishermen stored some of their catch in the old days and kept them fresh before using or sending off to market in the years before freezers were invented. It is well worth a visit to see a piece of Cresswell's fishing heritage which has stood the test of time and was fashioned and created by the fishing folk of Cresswell.

Cresswell Aero Base

An interesting article appeared in the Morpeth Herald in 1912. It states that Druridge Bay had been chosen as a North East Aero Base. The hangars and other structures were already in place. The site had been chosen because of the flatness of the terrain and isolation from other towns and villages. Soon flights would be trialled to confirm the suitability of the area. Indeed this did happen when Captain Sanderson flew his aircraft towards Cresswell and back again along the shoreline to the applause of the general public who turned out to watch. No indication as to the airfield's use after that time has come to light or the exact position of it.

During the First World War, Captain Louis Hall was a pilot with the Pioneer Corps. Local airfields were sited at Ashington and Cramlington where 36 Squadron were based for sometime and, at Ashington, an old building used for storing ammunition was discovered in 2012. After the war ended, local man Captain Hall put his bi-plane to good use when charging locals for short flights in his aircraft.

A field near to Kennels Cottage, Cresswell was the site used by Captain Hall to give joy rides to locals. He stands at the wingtip of his aircraft with a crowd of curious local children in the 1920s.

People Power

When the news that the building of a nuclear power station was being considered at Druridge Bay in 1978 it stirred a hornets' nest of protest from locals and several action groups. After many years of meetings, letter writing, protest marches and MPs' involvement, the scheme was eventually shelved and a lifeline given to what is the county's jewel in the crown. With a seven mile stretch of golden sands and a hinterland of important nature reserves, Druridge Bay at the present time remains a mecca for families, fishermen, birdwatchers, walkers and visitors to enjoy.

Right: A fine day in summer and Cresswell is the venue for many people to visit with a fine backdrop of dunes behind the clean white sands of the Long Bay. It is possible after the ebb of a spring tide to see the remains of an ancient forest that once existed here and extended from Chevington in the north to the south of the River Blyth.

At these times, a line of wooden poles can be seen that runs from the shoreline out into the sea and was once mooted as the site of an ancient village. These are only the remnants of a landing jetty where boats anchored when delivering limestone which was burnt in kilns sited along the dunes and used as a sweetner to the acid soil of the area.

Sand extraction from the bay started in 1945 to supply the building trade after the war. This practice was allowed to continue and by 1991 the bay had lost a substantial amount of sand. The Druridge Bay Campaign Group was set up to oppose not only a nuclear power station but sand extraction from the bay and were successful when the Northern Aggregates

Group pulled out in 1996. This picture shows how the sand was scraped from the beach then loaded into waiting wagons. However, permission still exists for sand extraction on a smaller scale.

The cairn at Druridge Farm set up during the action years for the public to lay a stone in support of the campaign opposing the building of a power station. At the rear are the marram grass dunes that circle the long Bay of Druridge.

The YMCA holiday camp at Cresswell in use from the early part of the 20th century until used by the military during the Great War and used as an internment camp for displaced persons in the Second World War. The Newcastle

based newspaper the Evening World organised a camp for kiddies and then Ashington Coal Company in 1932 organised a free holiday to young miners on a low wage. After the war years and the demise of Ashington Coal Company, it became a camp again controlled by the YMCA and then abandoned before becoming a caravan site. This picture is dated at the time of the Ashington Coal Company tenure.

Left: Only a wooden hut – the YMCA staff room – but kitted out with all the social amenities available. The organisation employed local girls in the every day running of the camp.

Below: Cresswell's long serving incumbent, the Rev Thomas Horsfall is among these young Boys' Brigade members parading and exercising on the beach in 1912.

Linton

The village and the early landowners and tenants are recorded way back in the 12th century. The De Balliol family owning much of the land at that time. The name of Linton is taken from the River Lin or Lyne, as we now know it, and the Saxon word for a dwelling which is tun or tonn. Evidence of the old rig and furrow method of farming and dating back to the middle ages has been identified at South Linton. Once part of the Widdrington Chapelry until the late 19th century, Linton is now an enclave of the Ellington Chapelry in the Ellington and Linton Parish. Without doubt a purely farming community until the sinking of Linton Colliery.

Joseph Chester arrived at the village in 1894 and recorded that Linton was a desolate place indeed with only a dozen houses built and four occupied. The one road in and out in winter was a mess of clay and water. The village affairs were handled by the Ellington Parish many of whom were farmers. They met once a year unless something urgent needed to be discussed. Mr Mavin of Linton Mill was assistant overseer of the village. The first parish council election was held on 17th March 1919, consisting of seven men, later increased to twelve.

More houses were added to the First, Second and Third Rows in 1899 and 1922 and this is when the Fourth and Fifth Rows were built. Electricity was added to homes in the First, Second and Third Rows in 1923. A Co-op was built in 1926 which is now the Post Office and Ingledene built and opened as Arnott's shop. Sammy the Jew built Holmdale which became a general dealers.

Dr Tom Skene was appointed doctor to the villages of Lynemouth, Linton and Ellington in 1923 and held early surgeries at a house in Linton's First Row.

In the early years, Ashington Coal Company banned alcohol from the village and it was 1937 before they allowed a small wooden hut to be built and used as Linton's Social Club.

Linton Colliery Miners' Welfare Institute

LINTON MINERS' WELFARE INSTITUTE

OPERATIC SOCIETY

(Under the auspices of the above Institute Committee)

WILL PRODUCE

"San Marino"

by permission of Curwen & Sons, Ltd.,

IN THE

Linton Welfare Hall

For four nights commencing **5th, 6th, 8th, 9th November, 1935.**

Each Night at 7·0 P.M.

CASTE :—

GENERAL MARTINEZ ... ... P. RIGG	RIQUETTE FRONSAC ... ... N. JACQUES
GASPER ... ... J. LEARY	ANNABEL SPINK ... ... MRS. TELFORD
CARLOS SANTEZ... ... ... J. TOMLIN	DOLORES ... ... MRS. CARMICHAEL
LUIS ... ... J. DAWSON	ROSITA ... ... R. DAWSON
DICKY TRAVIS ... ... P. SHOTTON	PEPITA... ... ... P. ALDERSON
PABLO ... ... H. JONES	CHEQUITA ... ... E. EMBLETON
HIRAM SPINK ... ... T. STRAUGHAN	FIRST PORTER ... ... J. TOMLINSON
LOLA GONSALEZ... ... ... P. EMBLETON	SECOND PORTER ... ... J. STRONG

Dancing troupe under Miss Watts.

Accompanists :—T. Fornear, J. Holland.   Producer :—R. Gustard.

CHORUS OF CITIZENS, PIRATES, SOLDIERS, ETC.

Tickets 1/- and **6d.** reserved if booked not later than 2nd November, 1935.

SURPLUS FUNDS IN AID OF INSTITUTE IMPROVEMENTS.

Wm. Thaxter, Hon. Sec.

A thriving Operatic Society existed in Linton and many of the original Linton families are represented here in the cast of 'San Marino' in 1935 at the Welfare Hall.

The Welfare Institute was opened on 29th October 1932 by Ebby Edwards, Secretary of the Mineworkers' Federation, and was very much the hub of the village. Built much later than the Lynemouth Institute, it was officially opened two years before the official Lynemouth premises were dedicated. Recreation included a large hall, cinema, billiards room and a cards room. There was a small sweet shop and a room used exclusively by ladies. The premises was also used as a doctor's surgery and baby clinic. Outside was a much used bowling green. Linton had a thriving Literacy Society, traced back to 1920. The English and Fornear families were prominent in this and members debated anything from politics to religion.

Linton Institute caretaker's house.

Co-op Guilds were found to be operating in most colliery villages and Linton was no exception. This photo is of the lady members in 1949.

Local exhibitors in the 1950s at a yearly flower show inspecting their stands of Dahlias with show judge, Wilf Turbill, second left of picture, looking on.

After the Second World War normality eventually returned to the community and Linton Youth Club soon organised trips to various venues. This one sees the members enjoying a day out at Rothbury about 1947.

In most pit villages you would find a lady who organised bus trips or holidays during the miners' annual leave and in Linton's case it was Mrs Robson. She is seen in the centre of picture with Linton residents who spent a week in Blackpool in the 1950s.

Linton Colliery

On the 1st April 1894, Mr Littlejohn cut the first sods for number one and two shafts. The two shafts fifty yards apart were sunk to a depth of 300 feet. The High Main Seam was found at 19 fathoms and the Yard Seam at 49 fathoms. William Alder was the master sinker and George Harrington, his assistant who was present when the first seam was found. Water was a continuous hazard and men wore sou'westers and buckskins. Water and the severe winter of 1895 delayed operations and it was July 1896 before the first coals were drawn from the pit. The new facility attracted

Linton Colliery

many workers from the old pits closing down around the county. Some settled in the five rows of houses built by Ashington Coal Company at Linton from 1898 until 1922. A number travelled to work from local villages while many lived at Ashington and travelled to work by the local tanky which pulled a set of workmen's carriages. This picture above shows the pithead in 1920 with coal production now well underway.

The discovery of former mining activity became apparent when miners holed into old mine workings in 1922 and found wooden sledges and crackets used by early miners. A filled in shaft was found no more than five foot in diameter and sunk to only 50 feet from the surface. This came as no real surprise as much evidence around the River Lyne of former coal extraction was well noted. This may have been by the monks of Newminster Abbey who had a living in Ulgham and were known to access coal for their own use from shallow pits.

On the 13th March 1926, Alderman William Weir opened the pithead baths. ACC director Leonard Milburn turned on the water and also in attendance were fellow directors, Francis Priestman and F.L. Booth. These baths were state of the art facilities with many improvements compared to the Ellington Baths opened two years earlier.

A separate canteen was built then and able to house 100 people.

Left: A major investment programme in the country's pits was carried out in the 1950s, including Ellington, Lynemouth and Linton Collieries. For Linton this meant a major modernisation and overhaul both on the surface and underground. This photo shows men working on the excavation for the new number two shaft headgear in April 1952.

A view from the south west side showing the building of the heapstead buildings and lamp room in May 1954.

October 1954 and the new heapstead and screens in process of erection with this view from the south. When completed, this is where the coal would be transferred from underground, screened then fed into wagons to be railed away to Ashington Washery.

1955 and looking east towards Ellington Colliery where the boiler house chimney and shaft towers are just visible in the background. In the foreground Linton's no 2 headgear, heapstead and screen house are complete and in operation. Coal can be seen in the wagons emerging from the screening plant.

Work on no 1 headgear and ancillary buildings began in January 1955. This picture shows construction work well underway on the shaft tower.

Right: A rare picture of a locomotive suspended in Linton's no 2 shaft before being lowered underground and housed in the loco shed to be prepared for haulage.

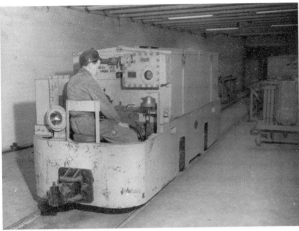

Safely lowered down the shaft, the 12 ton Logan Battery Locomotive is garaged and now being driven and assessed by electrical engineer, Stan Appleby.

This view shows the junction entrance to the loco house on left and the rail road to the shaft bottom. The laying out of the locomotive railroad from the inbye coal loading points to the shaft bottom meant coal could be transported quickly by locos pulling trains of mining cars, each with a capacity of holding two and a half tonnes.

It was often the case in colliery villages that sons followed fathers to work in the pits. It was expected in the early years by coal companies who were landlords of the miners' colliery houses. For the young men who showed promise academically,

they were given every opportunity to advance their education in mining by attending courses at Ashington Mining Continuation School. Linton student, Jim Miller, is standing far left with other students and teachers.

Many folk will remember the double gate crossings at Potland Signal Box which held up road traffic going to Linton Colliery and west to Longhirst when coal or passenger trains were due.

After the pit closed in 1968, and the running down of colliery rail traffic, the crossing gates were eventually taken away and replaced with automatic lights at the Potland crossing which spelled the end for the Potland signal box.

Wind of Change

While it is good to look back and remember how things used to be, those times have gone and can never happen again. We now live in a high tech world of computers, mobile phones and gadgets we never would have thought possible in bygone days. Coal from local collieries is no longer available locally since the closing down of the last North East pit at Ellington in 2005. Once king in the energy stakes, coal is now mined in local opencast sites and imported from abroad and is just a mere carbon footprint as green energy gradually takes over. Solar energy, wind power and possible clean energy extraction from untapped coal measures have become major factors in a bid for sustainable and renewable sources of power to help live our everyday lives. This is expected to be the way forward when supplies of North Sea oil and gas eventually diminish and opencast coal mining has run its course.

In December 2012 a Big Lottery grant of £1 million was allocated to the four villages of Linton, Lynemouth, Ellington and Cresswell. This sum, one of many given to deprived areas, is to be used in the coming years on projects identified by the villagers to promote facilities in the area.

Public meetings are taking place at each of the four villages and further consultation with those members who volunteered to commit their time to the project. Questionnaires were sent out to the public in 2013 so that they could have a say on how the money should be spent. At the time of writing some schemes have been agreed and acted upon with finance sought to kickstart the projects

Pictured at the CELL gazebo at Lynemouth Gala on 8th August 2015 these members of the CELL group are on hand to answer any queries concerning the various ongoing projects operating within the CELL villages of Cresswell, Ellington, Linton and Lynemouth. Left to right: Bill Tarbit, Pat McCann, Kevin Hindmarsh, John McCann and Gillian Mason.

On 22nd September 2015 an opening celebration was held at the First Bridge at the Lynemouth end of Ellington Dene. This was to mark the recent work by Groundworks UK who created an accessible and sound path into the Dene. Schoolchildren from Lynemouth William Leech Academy along with the Groundworks crew, Friends of the Dene, locals,

Co-ordinator Kevin Hidmarsh from the CELL group and members of Crown Estates part funders of the project. The Estates' representative, Andrew Wells, pictured fourth right officially opened the path.

Lynemouth schoolchildren went hands on at the opening ably guided by Dene project leader Leanne Shipley when they learned all about the flora and fauna.